Where do we go when we die? Or is there nowhere to go? Is death something we can do or is it just something that happens to us?

Now in his ninth decade, former Bishop of Edinburgh Richard Holloway has spent a lifetime at the bedsides of the dying, guiding countless men and women towards peaceful deaths. In *Waiting for the Last Bus*, he presents a positive, meditative and profound exploration of the many important lessons we can learn from death: facing up to the limitations of our bodies as they falter, reflecting on our failings and forgiving ourselves and others.

But in a modern world increasingly wary of acknowledging mortality, *Waiting for the Last Bus* is also a stirring plea to reacquaint ourselves with death. Facing and welcoming death gives us the chance to think about not only the meaning of our own life, but of life itself; and can mean the difference between ordinary sorrow and unbearable regret at the end.

Radical, joyful and moving, *Waiting for the Last Bus* is an invitation to reconsider life's greatest mystery by one of the most important and beloved religious leaders of our time.

WAITING
FOR THE
LAST BUS

Also by Richard Holloway

WAITING FOR THE LAST BUS

Reflections on Life and Death

RICHARD HOLLOWAY

CANONGATE

Published in Great Britain in 2018 by Canongate Books Ltd,
14 High Street, Edinburgh EH1 1TE

canongate.co.uk

1

Copyright © Richard Holloway, 2018

For permission credits please see p. 166

While every effort has been made to trace the owners of copyright
material reproduced herein, the publishers would like to apologise
for any omissions and will be pleased to incorporate missing
acknowledgements in any further editions

British Library Cataloguing-in-Publication Data
A catalogue record for this book is available on
request from the British Library

ISBN 978 1 78689 021 4

Typeset in Garamond MT by Palimpsest Book Production Ltd,
Falkirk, Stirlingshire

Printed and bound in Great Britain by Clays Ltd, St Ives plc.

Jeannie,
of course

The present life of men on earth, O King . . . seems to me to be like this: as if, when you are sitting at dinner with your chiefs and ministers in wintertime . . . one of the sparrows from outside flew very quickly through the hall, as if it came in one door and soon went out through the other. In that actual time it is indoors it is not touched by the winter's storm; but yet the tiny period of calm is over in a moment, and having come out of the winter it soon returns to the winter and slips out of your sight. Man's life appears to be more or less like this; and of what may follow it, or what preceded it, we are absolutely ignorant.

The Venerable Bede[1]

CONTENTS

I

THE DANCE OF DEATH

The medieval parish church of Saint Mary Magdalene in the town of Newark in Nottinghamshire, England, is a huge building, so you have to look carefully for one of its most interesting features. When it was built in the fifteenth century, England was a Catholic country obsessed with what happened to people after death. It was believed that where you went when you died depended on the kind of life you had lived on earth. For the perfect, for the saint who had lived a life of heroic virtue, there was the prospect of eternal life in heaven. For the wicked, there was the prospect of eternal damnation in hell. It was a dramatic choice between endless joy and unending torment. But the Church has always been good at finding ways to soften its harshest teaching. And that's what happened here.

In the thirteenth century, the Church invented a half-way house between heaven and hell called purgatory, from the Latin for 'place of cleansing'. Purgatory was a moral laundromat, where sinners who had soiled their souls on earth were slowly bleached of their stains and restored to purity. It was painful for them, but unlike the souls in hell, for whom there was never any hope of escape, the souls in purgatory had the prospect of release to cheer them on. And the assistance of the living was another source of encouragement. It was believed that the prayers of those still alive on earth could hasten the cleansing of those in purgatory. The best way to speed them on was to have masses said for them in special chapels called 'chantries', from the French for chanting. Chantry priests were recruited by wealthy families to pray their relatives through purgatory, much the way a lawyer for a guilty defendant might enter a plea of mitigation on their behalf in order to reduce their sentence.

In 1505, the prosperous Nottinghamshire Markham family built a chantry chapel inside Saint Mary Magdalene and hired a priest to say mass there. On the outside of the stone panels of the little chapel, they painted a favourite subject of medieval artists called the Dance of Death. One panel showed a dancing skeleton holding a carnation, a symbol of mortality. On the other panel there was a richly dressed young man clutching a purse. The skeleton's message to the young man was clear. As I am today, you will be tomorrow. And the money in your purse won't help you. It was a *memento mori,* a prompt to observers – remember you must die – to make them think about and prepare for their end.

It's a far cry from how we do things today. Now we spend a lot of time and effort *not* thinking about death. To face our own death is, quite literally, the last thing most of us will do – if we're conscious enough at the time to do it even then. Even if we wanted to, the chances are we won't have much control over how we leave the scene. Death and dying have been taken over by the medical profession; and there's a lot of evidence to suggest that it sees death not as a friend we might learn to welcome but as an enemy to be resisted to the bitter end. And the end often is experienced as bitter, as a fight we lost rather than as the coming down of the curtain on our moment on the stage, something we always knew was in the script.

People in the Middle Ages didn't have that luxury, if luxury it is. For them, life-threatening illness was as unpredictable and unavoidable as the weather, and they never knew when the lightning might strike. And, considering what came after, it made sense to be prepared for death. In contrast to health professionals today, who advise us to remember the dos and don'ts of healthy living in order to delay death as long as possible, the medieval Church was an advocate of healthy dying. It produced a guide on how to do it called *Ars moriendi* (*The Art of Dying*), a handbook for making a good end. Repenting and confessing your sins was the most important advice they gave the dying. And the reason why is captured by Hamlet in Shakespeare's most famous play. The young prince finds his hated stepfather at prayer and decides to kill him:

> Now I might do it pat, now he is praying;
> And now I'll do it: – and so he goes to heaven;
> And so am I revenged: – that would be scanned:
> A villain kills my father; and, for that,
> I, his sole son, do this same villain send
> To heaven.
> O, this is hire and salary, not revenge . . .

Up, sword, and know thou a more horrid hent:
When he is drunk asleep, or in his rage;
Or in the incestuous pleasure of his bed;
At gaming, swearing, or about some act
That has no relish of salvation in it, –
Then trip him, that his heels may kick at heaven;
And that his soul may be as damned and black
As hell, whereto it goes.[2]

The message was clear. If you die before you've had time to examine your conscience, own your guilt and confess your sins, you'll go straight to hell. And since you never know when the bell will summon you, the safest course is to be ready at all times, with your bags packed and your soul scrubbed clean. The other big piece of advice in *The Art of Dying* was about money. There are no pockets in a shroud, so you can't take your money with you when you die. But disposing of it wisely while you are alive will help you secure decent lodgings on the other side. And there was a saying of Jesus that confirmed the message: 'Use your worldly wealth to win friends for yourself, so that when money is a thing of the past you may be received into an eternal home.'[3] Those were the important messages packed into that little cartoon on the wall of the chantry chapel in Newark's parish church.

I had travelled to Newark on a golden September day to visit Kelham Hall, a few miles away on the banks of the River Trent. And I was wondering if it might be my last visit. I had been returning insistently over the years to prowl the grounds and remember my life there more than sixty years ago, then a young monk trying and failing to give his life away to God in a grand gesture of self-sacrifice. I knew this constant returning was an unhealthy obsession, but I couldn't shake it. The Victorian parson poet Charles Tennyson Turner had already warned me of the dangers of trying to recover lost time:

> In the dark twilight of an autumn morn,
> I stood within a little country town
> Wherefrom a long acquainted path went down . . .
>
> The low of oxen on the rainy wind,
> Death and the Past, came up the well-known road
> And bathed my heart with tears, but stirred my mind
> . . .
>
> But I was warn'd, 'Regrets which are not thrust
> Upon thee, seek not . . . thou art bold to trust
> Thy woe-worn thoughts among these roaring trees . . .
> Is't no crime
> To rush by night into the arms of Time?'[4]

These long-acquainted paths had witnessed great changes since I had lived there in the middle of the last century. Kelham Hall was no longer the home of a religious order that trained poor boys for the ministry of the Anglican Church. Now it was a stately hotel, and on the day of my visit it was hosting a large British Asian wedding. For the ceremony, the massive, domed chapel that had dominated my boyhood and haunted my dreams had been converted into a shrine to the Hindu God Ganesh. And it was filled with hundreds of joyful and colourfully dressed wedding guests. Did they catch the vibration of the hundreds of black-robed young men who had once tried to sacrifice themselves to God in this haunted space, now dominated by the friendly presence of the Elephant God? It certainly did not feel like it to me, but to my surprise this did not deepen my 'woe-worn thoughts'. It banished them. I was touched by the cheerful indifference of the wedding guests to the ghosts that whispered in my ear. Suddenly, something lifted in me. And I knew I wouldn't have to come back here again. What had been, had been. Now it was no more. I remembered Binyon's 'The Burning of the Leaves':

> Now is the time for stripping the spirit bare,
> Time for the burning of days ended and done,
> Idle solace of things that have gone before:
> Rootless hopes and fruitless desire are there;
> Let them go to the fire, with never a look behind.
> The world that was ours is a world that is ours no
> more.[5]

I decided to let the past go and turn to what was left of my future. I left Kelham happier than when I arrived. But the day's surprises weren't over.

The great tower of St Mary Magdalene dominated the flat Nottinghamshire landscape. I had been noticing it for most of my life, most recently from the train window on trips between Edinburgh and London. But I had never entered it, never seen what it was like inside. If my compulsive visits to Kelham were over, this was my last chance. So on my way to the station in Newark, I went in to look around and found that skeleton doing his dance of death.

It had an interesting effect on me when I saw it. It did not compel me to rush off to confession to purge my conscience of its sin, but it did remind me that I was speeding towards the final curtain. It made me think.

I had been taught to treat skeletons with respect while I was a curate in 1960s Glasgow by my Rector's son, a medical student who went on to become a distinguished physician in Africa. He had invited me to a student party and was disappointed when he discovered that one of his fellow medics had borrowed a skeleton from the anatomy lab and laid it in the bath to surprise visitors to the lavatory. I was amused by the prank till he reminded me that the skeleton had once been a pulsing, laughing human being. Someone had once known and loved this object of fun now lying in a bath in a student flat on Byres Road. Skeletons remind us that devouring time will get us all in the end. It has been reckoned that since we appeared on the planet there have been 107 billion human beings, 7 billion of whom are alive today. That means that the skeletons of 100 billion of us have faded into the earth. Occasionally we come across one that has been buried for thousands of years, and we wonder about the life it had, its joys, its sorrows and what it made of the world it found itself in.

I remember thinking about this when I first saw the famous photograph of human skulls at the Nyamata Genocide Memorial in Rwanda. In 1994, a million Tutsis were massacred by the forces of the Hutu-led government of Rwanda. Taken in 2007, the photograph shows a tray of some of the human skulls recovered from the killing fields, relics of one of the worst crimes of the twentieth century. It is the empty-yet-staring eye sockets that haunt the viewer. Vivid lives cut short; and the knowledge that, one way or another, we'll all come to this. We'll end as skeletons or as the ash of skeletons. 'As I am today, you will be tomorrow.'

And the process starts well before we die. It wouldn't be so wrenching if we never aged and didn't see death coming for us, with or without a machete in its hand. We'd run and laugh and climb mountains and dive into the sea with undiminished energy our whole life long. Then, at an unexpected moment when we were in the middle of our song, we'd be taken by death in the glory of our being – and it would be over in a second. That is not how our dance towards death usually goes. If we live long enough, we become witnesses to our own slow dying and the revelation of the skull beneath the skin. Psalm 90 says:

> The days of our age are threescore years and ten; and though men be so strong that they come to fourscore years; yet is their strength then but labour and sorrow; so soon passeth it away and we are gone.[6]

I have reached fourscore years, and though my life is not yet 'but labour and sorrow', I am aware that the shutting down of my body has begun. I am well into the last swing of the dance, and I can feel the beat quickening. That's what has prompted these reflections on being old and facing death.

I remember when I noticed that coloured patches like stains on old stone had started to appear on my face and body. When you get old, the garbage-disposal mechanisms designed to clear out waste in your skin cells start to break down. Instead of clearing the rubbish away, like lazy bin men they leave it lying around in the street, your skin. And it clots into those yellow-brown patches called '*lipofuscin*', better known as age spots. A few years ago at the Edinburgh International Book Festival, the press team photographed the writers with a special camera that subjected their skin to a ruthless high-definition exposure of every flaw and wrinkle. When my picture went up in Charlotte Square a few days later, it revealed a face blotched and stained with patches of *lipofuscin* even I hadn't noticed before. The bin men of my epidermis had obviously gone on permanent strike. That was when I realised that the wind-down of my body was well advanced and there would be more to come. Mind you, for me the process had started in my twenties, when I started going bald.

Baldness is not a terminal disease, of course, but it is a permanent condition. And I hated it when it started. I fought it in all the usual hopeless ways. I even bought pills advertised in a church magazine. The manufacturers probably thought the readers of *Church Illustrated* would have a stronger gift of faith than other baldies. Their pitch worked on me. I sent off for the pills. Nowadays the law would require an accurate description of the chemistry of the product that came through my letterbox a few days later, but none of that was required in 1958.

They looked like little brown Smarties. And like Smarties they were probably made of sugar. I started swallowing one a day. My hair continued to recede. Hopelessly, I flushed the remaining pills down the toilet and started combing what was left on top to the front, trying to look like Marlon Brando as Mark Antony in the movie *Julius Caesar* that was out at the time. It was a vain response to a disagreeable reality. It may delude the owner for a moment, but the comb-over is an embarrassment that takes no one in. Depressed yet defiant, one day I cropped the whole thing off and that's what I've done ever since. It was an early lesson in accepting things about myself I did not like but could not change. I see now that losing my hair was a good preparation for ageing and death, the skeleton being the ultimate baldy. Maybe I've been lucky to have had an early rehearsal.

My unsuccessful struggle with baldness taught me something about the human condition. Humans are afflicted with a tragic self-consciousness that does not seem to bother the other animals. All animals feel pain, but the one pain that seems to be unique to humans is an awareness of our bodies that is so keen it can lure us into depression and self-hatred. We are not only aware of our own bodies; we are aware of others' awareness of them. We are conscious of looking at others and being looked at by them. And we wonder what they make of what they see when they see us.

How did this obsession with our appearance start? Was it there before mirrors and cameras were invented? Would we be bothered by what we looked like if we couldn't see ourselves as others see us? However it started, our self-image seems to have obsessed us for centuries. The first-century Roman poet Ovid adapted an old Greek myth to explore the subject. Narcissus, the son of a river god and a local nymph, was famous for his beauty. The blind seer Tiresias warned his mother that Narcissus would have a long and happy life only if he never saw himself. Unfortunately, he caught sight of his own reflection in the waters of a spring, fell in love with what he saw and died of unrequited love.

If an experience has been developed into a myth like that, it is because its theme is universal. It expresses a reality that troubles the human community. This one suggests that we'd be better blind than obsessed with how we look, because it's a compulsion that can never be fully satisfied or appeased. Freud took the story further and coined the term *narcissism* for anyone suffering from an overpowering degree of self-esteem, a condition he diagnosed as a form of emotional immaturity. It is captured in the caricature of the egotist, usually a dominant male, who pauses in his narrative of self-glorification only long enough to say to his listener: 'But enough from me; tell me how you rate my accomplishments?' Narcissism in both its classic and Freudian forms has become a prevalent disease in late-modern societies obsessed with image and the screen technologies that promote it. It supplies the energy for one of the main enterprises of modern capitalism, the Anti-Ageing and Postponement of Death industry, what we might call the AAPD complex. We spend fortunes delaying death and the physical dissolution that precedes it.

And it starts early, with our revolt against the reality of the bodies we were born with. Had I been born sixty years later, would I have saved up for hair-transplant surgery rather than wasting my money on those wee sweeties advertised in *Church Illustrated*? And would I have missed learning one of the best lessons life teaches: that it is better to accept reality rather than deny it, including the reality of our own bodies and the death that is their only end? Throughout most of history, humans had no alternative but to accept these certainties. In our advanced techno-logical society, that is no longer the case. We spend fortunes trying to refashion our bodies and postpone our deaths. And it is easy to understand why. Anguish is a hard thing to bear, even if it is only the anguish of not liking the way we look. The anguish of dying is harder still, especially if it comes before we are ready for it, and we feel cheated of the time we thought we had left.

But there is no escape from anguish. It comes with the human condition and the self-awareness that is its key component. The secret is to learn how to live with it. Accepting the reality of the way we look and the certainty of our death, maybe one day soon, won't make us happy, but it might save us from the greater unhappiness of trying to ignore or hide from these realities. The fleeting pain of admitting our situation is preferable to the constant pain of denying it. It takes fortitude, the most useful of the old virtues. Fortitude is one of the most important lessons life teaches, and ageing may be our last chance to learn it. It is the ability to endure the reality of our condition without flinching. It was defined by the gay cowboy in the movie *Brokeback Mountain*: 'If you can't fix it, you gotta stand it.' And there's a lot you gotta stand when you get old.

Such as going deaf! It hasn't happened to me yet, but it has to my wife. What distresses me is that I find it irri-tating. Much of the time I have to shout to be heard by her, a small price to pay for close contact with someone I love. Yet it constantly annoys me. That says something to me about larger society as well as my own impatience. If we are not careful, we can start resenting the presence of the elderly in our midst and the minor irritations they impose upon the rest of us. Their deafness may annoy me, but the glacial way they move can induce bouts of sidewalk rage in me. The day will come when I'll walk more slowly too, but I'm still fleet of foot, so I get angered by those who hold up my progress along the street or through the aisles of the supermarket. I mutter to myself that they shouldn't be allowed out after the age of seventy unless they can pass a minimum-speed mobility test. For God's sake, why can't they get a move on? If I can have those terrible thoughts about the old in my eighties, I wonder how the millennial generation feels.

Worse than losing your hearing or your mobility is losing your short-term memory. Those moments when you can't find a name or forget what you were just about to say to someone. My wife and I joke that we have one good memory between the two of us. That's the best way to handle the ageing business – with a sense of humour, the blacker the better. In his nineties, my father-in-law stopped buying green bananas, because he didn't think he'd live to see them ripen.

Apart from humour, another source of consolation in old age is that vanity and self-consciousness fade away. In his memoir, the American novelist John Updike mused on how embarrassed he used to be by the hats his father wore when he was old. Then when he reached that time of life himself, he found himself wearing the same battered monstrosities. I too have a shelf full of embarrassing lids that I fancy give me a jaunty glamour. My wife tells me they just look daft. Well, daft it is. I shall embrace my inner scarecrow and agree with the Irish poet W.B. Yeats that:

> An aged man is but a paltry thing,
> A tattered coat upon a stick, unless
> Soul clap its hands and sing, and louder sing . . . [7]

It is possible to say a rueful 'Yes' to our fading energies and begin to appreciate the humour and understanding that old age can bring.

***

Much more difficult is giving up the prospect of the future. Not so much my own as that of my children and grand-children. Not to be there to see them make their way through life. And not just to see them. To be beside them when they hit sorrow, as they will, for no one misses it. To be someone they talk *about*, no longer someone they talk *to*. That's what the English poet Philip Larkin most hated about death. He described it as:

> . . . the total emptiness for ever,
> The sure extinction that we travel to
> And shall be lost in always. Not to be here,
> Not to be anywhere,
> And soon; nothing more terrible, nothing more true. [8]

Nothing more true, certainly, but why should it be so terrible? After all, we won't be there to know we're not there. When you're extinct you don't realise it, so it can't hurt. The Greek philosopher Epicurus said that fearing the not-being-there that follows death is as silly as regretting that we weren't here before we were born.

But it is not the thought of being dead that troubles us; it is the prospect of leaving and losing those we love that grabs us by the throat. And we already know something of what that feels like. Life has given us many anticipations of our dying. We only have to recall the memory of other separations to realise how wrenching the last one is going to be. The frail figure watching our car disappear round the bend before turning in at her lonely door; the moment in the station when we can't say goodbye because our heart is filling our throat, and we clutch hands and turn away.

> Someone is waving a white handkerchief
> from the train as it pulls out with a white
> plume from the station and rumbles its way
> to somewhere that does not matter. But
> it will pass the white sands and the broad sea
> that I have watched under the sun and moon
> in the stop of time in my childhood as I am
> now there again and waiting for the white
> handkerchief. I shall not see her again
> but the waters rise and fall and the horizon
> is firm. You who have not seen that line hold the
> brimming sea to the round earth cannot know this
> pain and sweetness of departure.[9]

Painful as these partings are, there may be the promise of future meetings to console us. And there are ways of keeping in touch with people we love that can compensate us for their distance. In dying, we face the final and absolute separation not only from those we love but from ourselves. Dying not only kills our bodies, it kills our future. I look at my grandchildren now in all their vivid promise, knowing I will miss seeing where their lives take them. And a quiet sorrow touches me. It doesn't overwhelm me, but as I gaze at them with pride and wondering affection I hear a distant bell toll. And I know it tolls for me.

In old age, this kind of rumination can make us feel sad about the future we are going to miss. But that shouldn't be the primary emotion we feel at the end of a long life. It should be gratitude. We won a rare lottery ticket when we were born. There must have been something in our DNA that beat the odds against fusing the sperm with the egg that made our particular existence possible. Millions did not make it off the wasteful assembly line in the great reproduction factory of life. We got through. We made it. For that at least we should be grateful; and even more grateful for the world that received and nurtured us; for the fact that it was there to receive us. I have known people who have died in a mood of absolute gratitude for the life they'd had and the love that was given to them. They were *sad* at leaving the party earlier than they hoped, but grateful for the good time they'd had while they were there. Their last days became an act of thanksgiving for what they had received.

There's an illuminating moment at the end of Alan Hollinghurst's novel, *The Line of Beauty*, which is set during the early days of the AIDS epidemic in Britain. Nick, the hero of the novel, has just had an HIV test. He knows the result will be positive and he'll die soon. Hollinghurst tells us:

> [Nick] . . . dawdled on rather breathless, seeing visions in the middle of the day. He tried to rationalize the fear, but its pull was too strong and original. It was inside himself, but the world around him, the parked cars, the cruising taxi, the church spire among the trees, had also been changed. They had been revealed . . . The emotion was startling . . . It was a love of the world that was shockingly unconditional. He stared back at the house, and then turned and drifted on. He looked in bewilderment at number 24, the final house with its regalia of stucco swags and bows. It wasn't just this street corner but the fact of a street corner at all that seemed, in the light of the moment, so beautiful.[10]

As death approaches, there will be sorrow for what it will take from us. But that is a mean and grudging way to greet it. If we let it, death will reveal the beauty of the world to us – *the fact of a street corner at all!* Maybe we have left it late. Maybe we wish we had noticed it before, paid it more attention. Push that thought aside. Don't fret. Look at it *now – so beautiful –* and be grateful. And maybe you can arrange your death bed looking out on a street corner you know . . .

II

LOSING IT

In his most famous poem, the Welsh poet Dylan Thomas advised his dying father not to give up without a fight:

> Do not go gentle into that good night,
> Old age should burn and rave at close of day;
> Rage, rage against the dying of the light.[11]

It is the rage of the old that I want to think about now. And not just the kind Dylan Thomas was talking about. That was rage at dying, at being dragged away from the party before you were ready to leave. There can be something heroic about that kind of resistance, and it is why some people, almost without being aware of it, fight hard against their own death. I have sat by the beds of many who were dying and marvelled at how long it was taking them to leave. Their relatives would be worn out sitting beside them day after day as they battled the inevitable. But the nurse in attendance always knew what was going on. He's a fighter, she would say. He won't let go till the last minute. It won't be long now. Then the moment of surrender would come: a last sigh and it was over.

This defiant resistance of death seems to be stronger

in some people than in others, part of their character. And the will to live can persist in them long after they've lapsed into a coma. I'm always moved when I see this happening. It suggests to me an event in the boyhood of the writer Leonard Woolf when he was told to drown five new-born puppies:

> When he plunged the first tiny blind creature into the bucket of water, it began 'to fight desperately for its life, struggling, beating the water with its paws.' He suddenly realised that it was an individual, an 'I', and that it was fighting for its life just as he would, were he drowning.[12]

Like those blind puppies, death's resisters struggle against the forces that are shutting them down. It's hard not to be moved by this. It is probably the energy that kept them going as long as they did. But they all have to give in at some point. Death gets everyone in the end. If it didn't, life would soon become unsustainable on our little planet. And there are worrying trends already pointing in that direction.

One of them is the way the medical profession has wheeled formidable new artillery onto the battlefield and spends vast amounts of money and effort delaying death's victory. I don't apologise for the military metaphor because it is the one favoured by doctors themselves. With the best of intentions, they have taken control of the lives of old people today, and they fight hard to keep them in the field as long as possible. The result for many of them is a medicalised existence whose sole purpose is staying alive long after any joy in doing so has fled.

Keeping most of us alive well into our eighties is one of the successes of modern medicine, but there are signs it is having a profoundly distorting effect on the balance of society as a whole. In Britain, the care of the elderly is close to swamping the resources of the National Health Service, turning it into an agency for the postponement of death rather than the enhancement of life. We don't have to go back to the fifteenth century to find a more balanced approach. Not that long ago, before they had this colossal armoury at their disposal, most doctors were willing to acknowledge death's approach. They saw their role as helping death in with the minimum of distress to everyone. Nowadays they are more likely to call in the medical engineers to dig a moat and fortify the door against death's entrance. But there are signs that the more thoughtful among them are beginning to challenge this siege mentality. The American physician Atul Gawande has recently suggested that while medicine exists to fight death and disease, it should learn how to fight for territory that can be won and how to surrender it when it can't. And doctors need to understand that the damage is greatest if they insist on battling on to the bitter end.[13]

Old age can be bitter if it is experienced not as a period of calm preparation for death but as a grim battle to keep it at bay. It can even breed resentment in the old against the very doctors who are working hard to keep them going. Visiting the elderly can be a dispiriting experience if they spend the time rehearsing their ailments and complaining about the inattention of the local health professionals who are run off their feet trying to care for them. The reality is that death has rung their bell, and peace will come only when they open the door and say you got here sooner than I expected, but come in and sit down while I get my coat on.

***

If the refusal to accept the imperative of death is a relatively new phenomenon, an older affliction is the anger of the old at the young for being young. At its root this is one of the many forms of the sin of envy. Envy has been defined as sorrow at another's good. Sometimes it is confused with jealousy, but there's a world of difference between them. The jealous want what other people have, and it may provoke them to work hard to achieve it, which is why 'keeping up with the Jones's' is a proverb. Jealousy may drive us to action, but envy only makes us depressed. Rather than rejoicing in the happiness of others – their youth and vitality and beauty – it makes us sad. It can prompt bitterness towards the young for being young, revealed in the snort of contempt at how they colour their hair or tattoo their bodies or collide with you in the street because *they're always on their bloody phones*. It's an ugly picture, the face of angry, envious old age. We often see it on television during interviews with the public on the issues of the day; and it can have a solid impact on government.

Elderly voters are a powerfully reactionary force in politics both in the United Kingdom and in the United States. They are more disciplined and consistent than the young in voting, so as they increase in size as a cohort of the population their envies and resentments are bound to have an increasingly distorting effect on political processes. There is already a lot of evidence that they have had a profound effect on recent elections and referenda in these two countries. If these trends continue, in a few years a number of western democracies will have transformed themselves into gerontocracies – governments of the old, by the old, for the old. Geriatric resentment is a dangerous disease to catch, so it's worth examining ourselves to see if it has infected us.

The chances are that we've caught it, if only a mild version, because it is hard to avoid. Each generation has to learn how to take a bow and leave the stage. And we have to do it at the time in our lives when we are least resilient. Old age is a poignant business, a continuous series of losses, which is why Bette Davis said it wasn't for sissies. One of its saddest moments is when we realise we are no longer at home in the world and are baffled at how it operates. When we were young and the future was filled with promise, it was thrilling to celebrate the constant shift and change of history and embrace every fad that came off the assembly line, as well as being impatient with those who resisted the new and clung desperately to the old and outworn. It is a different matter when you realise that, almost without noticing it, you have joined the ranks not only of the old but of the old fashioned; and that the crazy shifts of change you embraced so eagerly when you were young are the very energies that are now carrying you into the past, along with steam trains and quiet Sundays. So it is hardly surprising that the old can begin to feel like strangers in their own land.

But it's a mistake to think it's a modern disease. The bitter old person is a constant in history. It seems to be age that corrodes the spirit, not change as such, which is why growing old can be spiritually dangerous. Go back as far as you can and you'll hear the old grumbling about the young. In the century before the birth of Christ, the Roman poet Horace heard an elderly man at it:

> Tiresome, complaining, a praiser of the times that were when he was a boy, a castigator and censor of the young generation . . .[14]

The tone of these attacks on the younger generation is not always as angry as Horace's old man. Sometimes it is reproachful and weary, a wry shaking of the head at the excesses of the young. This is the spirit of Alec Guinness's memoir, *A Positively Final Appearance*. The famous film star even complains about the length of movies nowadays:

> What good stories were told in the cinema in those days, swiftly, directly and without affectation. And how blessedly short they were when compared to the three-hour marathons that we are now expected to sit through, with aching bums, fatigued eyes and numbed ears.[15]

Behind these complaints and reproaches there is hurt and sadness at the way time sweeps each generation aside, famously expressed by Isaac Watts in his hymn, 'O God, our help in ages past':

> Time, like an ever-rolling stream,
> Bears all its sons away;
> They fly forgotten, as a dream
> Dies at the opening day.[16]

That it is a Christian hymn that best describes the rush of remorseless time is no accident. Religion is one of the few institutions that keeps the thought and fact of death steadily before us. It is what intrigued the poet Philip Larkin about churches. That so many dead lay round them, he thought, made them 'proper to grow wise in'.[17] But you don't need a burial ground round a church to be reminded of death. There are reminders inside as well. Being a member of a congregation is to watch chairs emptying, as death accomplishes its work. In John Meade Falkner's poem, 'Christmas Day: The Family Sitting', an old man in church meditates on Christmases past:

> There are passed one after the other
> Christmases fifty-three,
> Since I sat here with my mother
> And heard the great decree:
> How they went up to Jerusalem
> Out of Galilee.
>
> They have passed one after the other;
> Father and mother died,
> Brother and sister and brother
> Taken and sanctified.
> I am left alone in the sitting,
> With none to sit beside . . .
>
> The pillars are twisted with holly,
> And the font is wreathed with yew
> Christ forgive me for folly,
> Youth's lapses – not a few,

For the hardness of my middle life,
For age's fretful view.[18]

Nowadays, sitting in church, I am often more aware of
the presence of the dead than of the living. I remember
where they sat, a hymn they loved – sung again this
morning – and maybe the bitterness of their passing. But
it is a fortifying not a depressing experience, a reminder
that this is how it goes, and that I must be reconciled to
it. One day my seat will be empty, and my name will be
written among the dead. Going to church is one of the
ways I gather the past round me as I prepare to go up to
Jerusalem out of Galilee. But it has become a more complicated business than it used to be. For many old people
today, going to church can be an alienating rather than a
consoling experience. To understand why will take a bit
of thinking about religion itself.

***

The best way to see religion is as humanity's response to
the puzzle of its own existence. Unlike the other animals
on earth, we have never felt entirely at home here. Our big
brains prompt us not only to wonder about our own existence but about the existence of existence itself. Is there a
reality behind it that created it, and can we relate to it in
any way? Some of us think compulsively about these questions and come up with a stream of never-very-certain
answers. The instrument we use for wrestling with them is
the human mind. Our difficulty is that we can't really be
certain *anything* exists outside the mind, because the mind

is the main agent we have for examining the question. The Cambridge theologian Don Cupitt tells us there is a German word that captures the difficulty, *unhintergehbarkeit,* 'unget-behindability'.[19] Our knowledge of the universe comes to us through the mind. And we can't get out of it or off it to prove *anything's* behind it – *or nothing's behind it* – except through the mind itself! We are stuck in and with our minds. And even if we want to resist that claim, it is only our minds that can challenge it thereby proving the point.

Living with the 'ungetbehindability' of the universe is frustrating, which is why we search for ways to resolve our predicament, either by convincing ourselves there is definitely nothing behind it, or there's definitely something and we've met it. Since it is impossible to prove the truth of a negative factual statement – *there's no one there* – absolute atheism only ever appeals to a passionate minority. But those who insist that there is someone there can't prove it either. What they offer is testimony or witness. Religion's most interesting characters are those who claim to have encountered the mystery behind the universe *directly.* They claim to have seen or heard it. It revealed itself to them. An example from within the Christian tradition is the French religious and mathematical genius, Blaise Pascal. After his death, a paper was found stitched into the lining of his coat that recounted a mystical experience he'd had on 23 November 1654. This is what was written on the scrap of paper:

FIRE. God of Abraham, God of Isaac, God of Jacob, not of the philosophers and scholars. Certainty. Certainty. Feeling. Joy. Peace.[20]

The fact that he told no one about the encounter was unusual, because religious witnesses usually want to share what they have seen or heard. Sometimes they attract followers, and another religion is born from their revelations. Pascal kept to himself what had happened, but it changed his life. It took him from *thinking* about God – *not of the philosophers and scholars* – to an encounter *with* God.

For those like Pascal, who claim to have been taken behind the veil of the universe, the experience is self-authenticating. Doubt is eradicated. Certainty. Certainty. That's why they are so persuasive. There is nothing like absolute conviction to persuade others to go along with you. But for those who go along – unless they are mystics themselves – doubts about the meaning of the original encounter always remain. To use one of Pascal's own descriptions, their faith is a gamble. The followers of a revelation are called 'believers' or 'people of faith'. And doubt is part of the deal. That's why faith is often characterised as a struggle. The faithful are told to pray to have their faith strengthened, a form of words that gives the show away. We don't pray to have our grasp of facts strengthened. We don't pray to believe more firmly in the two times table. We *know* it's true. We can do it on our fingers. Faith is different. By definition, it is tinged with uncertainty. This is fine for individuals, but it doesn't work for religious organisations, especially if they are keen on marketing themselves to unbelievers. Doubt doesn't sell; certainty does. The organisers who systematise a religion based on the experience of a prophet have a product to sell, and they know diffidence won't move the goods. That is why as religions develop they shift from exhortations to *faith* to proclamations of *fact*, including confident descriptions of the world or worlds behind the one that is available to our senses, the one our minds connect us to.

That is how the big theistic religions started, and by the time they reach us hundreds of years later, their original claims are beyond any definitive investigation or interrogation. That is why they become the source of endless, irresolvable disagreements about their truth. Rival schools of interpretation battle each other over the meaning of the original revelation. And because of the 'ungetbehind-ability' factor, there is no arbiter on earth who can resolve their disagreements. So they jostle and collide with each other like logs of timber on time's ever-rolling stream as it carries them through history.

But while this is going on, something else is happening at the same time. To capture it, I'll have to shift from a fluvial to an arboreal metaphor. Religions gradually thrust themselves above their mystical origins into real history, where they stand like huge trees able to shelter many different forms of attachment and meaning in their branches. Though they still claim to be rooted in the eternal world, in *this* world they represent values that are helpful to many who have little interest in the supernatural claims they make about their origins. For faith systems to let themselves be used in this way requires a tolerant generosity that appears to be under threat today.

I am writing this a few days before Christmas. For weeks the shops have been jingling with carols, and the streets have been decked with lights. And I enjoy it. Scotland is a cold dark place in the middle of winter. So I can understand why the ancient pagans cheered themselves up with a winter festival that reminded them the days would lengthen soon and spring would start its slow trail north. I can also understand why the Christian Church decided the pagan festival was a great idea and called it Christmas, a theft that would be dismissed today as cultural appropriation, forgetting that we've always borrowed from each other to help us through life's dark nights. Christmas is the one time of the year when churches will be packed. Almost in spite of themselves, people are drawn to sing carols and hear the story of a baby laid in a manger because there was no room in the inn. This is how C. Day Lewis described it in a poem:

It is Christmastide. Does the festival promise as fairly
As ever to you? 'I feel
The numbness of one whose drifted years conceal
His original landmarks of good and ill.
For a heart weighed down by its own and the world's
folly
This season has little appeal.'

But tomorrow is Christmas Day. Can it really mean
Nothing to you? 'It is hard
To see it as more than a time-worn, tinsel routine,
Or else a night incredibly starred,
Angels, oxen, a Babe – the recurrent dream
Of a Christmas card.'

You must try again. Say 'Christmas Eve'. Now quick,
What do you see?
'I see in the firelit room a child is awake,

Mute with expectancy
For the berried day, the presents, the Christmas cake.
Is he mine? or me?'

He is you and yours. Desiring for him tomorrow's
Feast – the crackers, the Tree, the piled
Presents – you lose yourself in his yearning, and borrow
His eyes to behold
Your own young world again. Love's mystery is revealed
When the father becomes the child.

'Yet would it not make those carolling angels weep
To think how incarnate Love
Means such trivial joys to us children of unbelief?'
No. It's a miracle great enough
If through centuries, clouded and dingy, this Day can keep
Expectation alive.[21]

It is poetry that draws people into church at the end of December to gaze again at 'the recurrent dream of a Christmas card'. The paradox is that it is the people who think religion is prose who keep it alive for the people who can only use it as poetry. When a religion is in decline, its prose becomes more defensive and assertive. But if it is not careful it loses the capacity for what the poet John Keats called 'Negative Capability':

. . . that is when man is capable of being in uncertainties, Mysteries, doubts, without any irritable reaching after fact and reason.[22]

Its very existence now threatened, the Church is in danger of becoming a club for strict believers who have little tolerance for religious versions of Negative Capability. And it can be devastating for elderly parishioners, whose practice of faith always owed more to John Keats than to Billy Graham. One of the features of my latter years is to be invited to speak to groups of people who think of themselves as the Church in Exile. Most of those who turn up are about my own age or only slightly younger. They are all people who have stopped attending church because they find the new, assertive tone impossible to bear. The growing congregations, the versions that attract the young, have learnt the old lesson that certainty sells and conviction satisfies. They have the vibrancy of student societies – high on their own virtue – who have gathered together to fortify themselves against their enemies. It can be devastating for the mildly religious, for whom religion was once a source of spiritual comfort and moral challenge, to be told there is now no room in the inn for doubt and uncertainty. I know a woman who was told by her new minister that her late father, an old-fashioned Presbyterian of the post-war liberal variety, was now in hell, and he would remain there for ever because he had not been born again into the version of Christianity that was now in the ascendant.

So added to the losses that accumulate in old age can be sorrow at the loss of the Church itself. And it's a double sorrow. There is the private sorrow of being exiled from the Christian community because it has no room for the wistful children of unbelief. There is the larger sorrow of seeing the presence of the Church slowly fade from the national landscape and become just another sect among many, all marketing themselves as the only true route to eternal salvation. The symbol of this larger sorrow is the sight of old churches that survive only as monuments to loss.

Our landscape is dotted with them, mute reminders of a time when the Christian faith was practised with generous confidence throughout the land. Seeing them closed and shuttered can prompt sombre reflection even in those who had little use for them in their glory. This is the mood of the poem 'Church Going' by Philip Larkin, from which I have already quoted. Larkin is out cycling in the country-side when he comes across an old church and goes in. He notices the 'little books; sprawlings of flowers, cut / For Sunday, brownish now . . . and a tense, musty, unignorable silence'. And he wonders what will happen to what he calls these serious houses on serious earth when they have all fallen out of use. He writes:

> I wonder who
> Will be the last, the very last, to seek
> This place for what it was . . . [23]

Before churches close their doors for the last time, they undergo a rite called de-consecration. It's a kind of funeral in which the sacredness is removed and the church becomes just another building. I know a handsome church that went through this process. It was one of the biggest churches in Gorbals in Glasgow when I lived there in the 1960s, sitting proudly in the midst of a teeming neigh-bourhood of grey tenements. I went in search of it not long ago, wondering if I'd be able to find it among the new streets and houses that have replaced the district I knew fifty years ago. I needn't have worried. Its new setting makes it more dominant than ever. Still a thrilling building, it is now way out of proportion to its new surroundings. And it is no longer a church.

St Francis Catholic Church and Friary, built by Pugin and Pugin in 1870, was dramatically decorated in the high Gothic style, and the enormous congregation was served by a team of Franciscan Friars. I remember hundreds of parishioners thronging into it for the Stations of the Cross in Holy Week. The vividly painted Stations are just about all you can see of the interior now. The church was sold in 1996 and converted to a conference and community centre by the insertion of a three-storey suite of rooms into the interior. It was disconcerting to stand in the church knowing that behind the screens the original arrangements were all as they had been in the past, as if waiting for the day when they would be unveiled and restored to their former glory.

The superintendent took me behind the elegant timber frame of the insertion to show me the high altar. He told me they still had a mass there once a year. He asked if I'd like to see the little chapel the Friars once used for their community worship. We went up a short flight of stairs, and he opened a little door. I stepped into a perfectly preserved small chapel. Next to the altar, a little window opened above the nave of the church. I looked down into the great space, imagining multitudes praying, lighting candles, whispering their sins into the ears of priests in brown habits, kindling faith into flame. I was hit by a sorrow that stayed with me long after I had thanked my guide and left the church. It was partly remembrance of my own young manhood in this place fifty years before, partly dismay at the way time hurtles so many good things into the past without a backward look. So I had to remind myself that the story of religion, like everything else in life, is one of constant change and loss.

The Pagans were heartbroken when Catholic Christianity arrived in Britain in the sixth century, and banished their gods and took over their temples. At the Reformation in the sixteenth century, the Catholic Church that had supplanted Paganism was pushed out of Britain. Protestantism took over, and a way of life that had its own beauty and romance was destroyed. In our day, it seems to be Christianity itself that is fading away. I can understand why, but it still hurts me. That's why, like Larkin, I derive a melancholy pleasure from visiting these old shrines and imagining their glory days.

***

What I can't mourn is 'the moral decay of Britain' that faith leaders tell us is an inevitable consequence of the decline of religion. Moral change isn't always decay. Sometimes it's an improvement. I can look back with sadness on the vanished churches of my youth. I don't mourn the passing of some of the moral attitudes they represented. The big moral shifts during my lifetime have all been improvements. I am thinking about the place and status of women and sexual minorities today, compared to how they were when I was young. If I were a woman or gay, I'd rather be alive in Britain now than in the Britain of my boyhood. Religious communities did little or nothing to bring about these improvements, because their sacred texts opposed them. It's hard to change an ancient prejudice if you have been taught that God commanded it.

One of the useful purposes of religion in the past was the way it reinforced society's moral order by hallowing it with divine authority. Inevitably, it overdid the reinforcement. Stable societies benefit from operating a moral consensus that most of their citizens accept. But for everything to stay the same, everything has to change. For society to keep itself together and endure through time, it has to respond to the creative dynamism of the human mind and its constant search not only for new ways of making things but for new ways of ordering its moral economy. Ethics, like everything else, is subject to change. That's why we should hold our values and moral norms with a sense of their provisional nature. We never know when we'll want to change them because we have been persuaded there is a better way to organise society:

> For every static world that you or I impose
> Upon the real one must crack at times and new
> Patterns from new disorders open like a rose
> And old assumptions yield to new sensation . . . [24]

Revealed religions find this hard to deal with. Their authors have persuaded them that they are in possession of a divine instruction that, unlike everything else in human history, isn't subject to change and decay. It's a mountain not a river. It stays put and never moves. That's why the biggest junk yard in history is the one marked Abandoned

Religions, abandoned because they were incapable of adapting to the flowing currents of human history.

To be fair to them, some Christian groups have tried to keep abreast of the currents of human history, but they have always been double-minded about it: one of their minds telling them to rope themselves to the mountain of eternal truth, the other telling them to throw themselves into the river of time and enjoy the swim. That's why they were late in joining the campaign to emancipate women and sexual minorities, two of the great moral causes of my lifetime. That resistance to change is one reason for their decline amongst many young people today. The so-called millennial generation, both in the UK and in the USA, is the least religiously committed cohort of the population there has been in the last sixty years, so the future for organised religion does not look promising. There is still a spiritual hunger and interest among the young, but they show a marked contempt for institutions which claim that they alone can perfectly satisfy it.

It's tough for believers to know how to respond to this situation, and I have sympathy for their predicament. They are fighting to stay afloat in the rushing flood of time. And the myth of the golden and untroubled past is always a potent attraction to those who have lost their moorings. Hence the busy reactionary churches many of us no longer feel at home in. As a tactic, it'll probably work for a while. It just doesn't work for me. But that doesn't matter. I won't be around to see how it plays out in the long run. I feel sad about that, but only a little. There are places where I can still find some spiritual comfort.

If, like me, you cannot halt the search for meaning in a

universe that does not explain itself; but if, also like me, you can no longer cope with the compulsive chatter of what E.M. Forster called 'poor little talkative Christianity'; then find a place where they don't talk, they sing – and leave your soul unmolested for an hour. Slip into choral evensong somewhere to experience the music and touch the longing it carries for the human soul. For that, you may have to find a cathedral, which brings us to a significant fact. In Britain today, cathedrals are among the places of worship that continue to thrive in an era of religious decline. There are doubtless a number of reasons for this, but I am sure that one of them is the fact that cathedrals are spiritually and theologically more spacious and welcoming than most parish churches. And as well as music, they have more quiet corners to sit in where you can avoid recruiters out to press-gang your mind. Cathedrals are perfectly apt for the complicated times we live in. I am fully aware of the paradox here. I have mentioned it already. It is those who believe in the prose of religion who keep it alive for those of us who can now only survive on its poetry. I just hope they'll go on saving that space for me a little longer. I am weary of the argument I've been engaged in all my life with religion and its volatile certainties.

What I want to do with what time I have left is to cherish those I love and indulge myself in that delicious form of reflective sadness we call melancholy. There are many ways to do it. The easiest is with an old friend or colleague over a meal and a bottle of wine, when you both look back. It has been said that the past is another country. Well, visit it in your memory, explore its foreignness, and see how different you were then. Be embarrassed by that other self, but be forgiving too. None of us really knew what we were doing. We were making it up as we went along; trying to figure it out; get the hang of it; find ourselves. Smile as you remember the way it was back then. Shake your head, but be kind.

And call up the dead. Remember them with fondness as well as exasperation. Their stories are over, so it's okay to try to assess them or reach a verdict on them. Don't be too hard on them. They were less sure of themselves than they seemed. It's not only the past that's another country. Most of our friends were strangers to us as well. They all had their own secrets and sorrows. The truth is, like us, they were fumbling their way through life. They were all a wee bit lost. So tenderness is all. They can't change their story now. It's told.

Ours isn't. Not quite. But maybe it's time to turn our mind towards our own ending, which might not be that far away. The bus might already have left the depot. As we begin to contemplate the end of our own story, it is important to get in the right mood. The mood I recommend is the last day of the holidays – another summer gone, and the sweet sadness of leaving. Poets do reflective melancholy better than anyone else, another reason the old should read them religiously as they close the story of their lives. Here's a poem that captures the mood I recommend: 'Goodbye to the Villa Piranha' by Francis Hope:

> Prepare the journey North,
> Smothering feet in unfamiliar socks,
> Sweeping the bathroom free of sand, collecting
> Small change of little worth.

Make one last visit to the tip
(Did we drink all those bottles?) and throw out
The unread heavy paperback, saving
One thriller for the trip.

Chill in the morning air
Hints like a bad host that we should be going.
Time for a final swim, a walk, a last
Black coffee in the square.

If not exactly kings
We were at least *francs bourgeois*, with the right
To our own slice of place and time and pleasure,
And someone else's things.

Leaving the palace and its park
We take our common place along the road,
As summer joins the queue of other summers,
Driving towards the dark.[25]

III

LOOKING BACK

Most of us were brought up to believe we made ourselves and constructed our own destiny. God – or the universe – had given us the freedom to choose the actions that would define our characters. We could choose to be good or bad, faithful or unfaithful, brave or cowardly. When the moment of trial came, we could choose to stand fast or run away. The short-hand term for this belief is 'free will'. The idea behind it is that each of us has agency or control over our lives. Whatever we did at any particular moment, we could have done the opposite, chosen differently. It was entirely up to us. Our actions were freely willed decisions.

And it is not just a piece of theory, a philosophical issue we debate. It has solid consequences in the way societies have ordered themselves for centuries. It lies behind the criminal-justice systems we have developed. It is why we build prisons and incarcerate people in them because of the crimes they freely chose to commit. It is why people have been stoned, flogged, beheaded, burned at the stake or drowned on ducking stools for forbidden practices they freely chose to take part in. In societies where the cruellest penalties have been abandoned, they have been replaced by public shaming in newspapers or social media, psychological ordeals that can be even more painful than physical punishment. As we say of those we punish: it serves them right; they got what they deserved.

As well as these external punishments, and the public blaming and shaming that go with them, individuals have internalised society's belief in free will deep within their psyches, where it prompts them into a wide repertoire of self-punishment. Disappointed at their own behaviour, they go through life burdened with guilt and self-hatred. And it can darken their final years as they look back at what they have made of themselves:

> I am gall, I am heartburn. God's most deep decree
> Bitter would have me taste: my taste was me . . . [26]

A friend of mine who is an expert on Norse folk tales wrote an essay that challenged this understanding of free will. In the essay, she explored the metaphor of weaving cloth on a loom as a better way of thinking about how our lives develop and our characters are formed. The metaphor suggests that we were more passive than active in the movement of our lives. *We* were never in charge. The weaver was. Another name for her is inheritance. She gathered the threads already formed by our DNA, and all the other circumstances that went into the making of our unique existence, and slowly wove them into the story of our life. The threads shuttled across the loom of time, and our portrait was gradually revealed. And by old age the picture is nearly complete, apart from a few threads yet to be tied up to finish the story. The Danish philosopher Søren Kierkegaard said that though we live our lives forwards, we can only understand them backwards when they are nearly complete. But even the perspective of old age cannot give us the complete picture – because the loom is still moving, and there is still time for a final twist to its pattern. Here's how Kierkegaard put it:

> It is perfectly true, as philosophers say, that life must be understood backwards. But they forget the other proposition, that it must be lived forwards. And if one thinks over that proposition it becomes more and more evident that life can never really be understood in time because at no particular moment can I find the necessary resting place from which to understand it.[27]

Kierkegaard's 'resting place' sounds a bit like Cupitt's 'ungetbehindability', the impossible place outside our lives, the only place from which we could see them in the round to justly evaluate them. Maybe Kierkegaard thought death would be 'the necessary resting place from which to understand' them, but since we won't be there to do the understanding when we are dead, the best perspective will be to get as close as we can to death and look back from there.

But what if we dislike what we see? What if we compare the person we turned out to be with the person we wanted to be and are disappointed at the difference? The performance is over, the curtain is closing, and there can be no encores. What if we give ourselves a bad review? That can be tough. Here's how the poet T.S. Eliot describes how the old can feel as they look back at events in their lives that now fill them with dismay:

> And last, the rending pain of re-enactment
> Of all that you have done, and been; the shame
> Of motives late revealed, and the awareness
> Of things ill done and done to others' harm . . . [28]

In the medieval *Ars moriendi* (The Art of Dying) that we looked at in the first chapter, the essential element was self-examination followed by confession to a priest and absolution, all designed to keep the soul out of hell. But there was probably more to it even then than a desperate act of self-protection before it was too late. It would have had earthly benefits as well. It might have healed damaged relationships and brought peace at the end, as the final threads were drawn together and the life was completed.

Whatever our views on religion and its rituals, that is still a wise approach to our end. And the re-enactment of all we have done and been need not result in Eliot's rending pain. The Norse folk tale of the weaver and the loom will give us a more generous perspective than squinting at ourselves through the narrow lens of the doctrine of free will. The ways we acted, the decisions we took, all revealed the kind of person we were predestined to be – because we were never as free as we thought we were. From the beginning, we were being driven by facts and circumstances that were never in our control. But it is important to get the attitude right here. In our self-examination, we are neither to blame nor to make excuses for ourselves: we are to try to understand. It's a bit like reading a compassionate biography that tries to show how the subject came to be the person she or he was. Ah, we say, that's where all that came from, that explains it.

Achieving an objective perspective on the self is hard, but it's worth the effort. Yes, we have to say, that's who I was, that's what I did. No point now in wishing I had been someone else, someone who didn't fall apart under pressure, someone who did not betray a loved one, a better parent, a more loving spouse. For better or for worse, that's who I was. That's why the view from the summit of life can be challenging. As death approached them, I have sat at the bedside of people eaten up with regret because of mistakes they made in their lives. Wrong roads they took; relationships broken and still unrepaired; troubled children who blamed them for their own failures. Looking back from old age can add an extra burden to what is already a difficult time. So I want to suggest a way to take some of the pain out of regret. And I want to begin by looking at a great painting from the seventeenth century.

The painting is *Peter the Penitent* by the Italian artist Guercino. It was painted in 1639 and now hangs in the National Gallery of Scotland. It shows Saint Peter the Apostle, his face stricken with anguish moments after his betrayal of Jesus. Peter's betrayal is a well-known story, but it's worth thinking about again for what it can teach us about human nature. Peter was an impulsive man, a loudmouth who was always protesting his devotion to Jesus. As it became obvious that Jesus's challenge to the religious and political authorities had placed him in danger of arrest for sedition and blasphemy, Peter got louder in his chest-beating. Everyone else may desert you, Master;

I never will. I'd rather die than forsake you. So I say to those coming for you, bring it on! If you want Jesus, you'll have to go through me first. And it wasn't just boasting. Peter meant what he said. That's what he intended to do. Because that was the kind of man he thought he was – or wanted to be.

The secret police came for Jesus in the middle of the night, the way they always do, and they took him away to try him, his death sentence already written. Peter followed, staying in the shadows, watching what was happening. Three times in the hours that followed he was challenged to admit he was a friend of Jesus. And three times he denied it, each denial louder than the one before. 'I DO NOT KNOW THIS MAN,' he finally screamed at them. The Gospel of Luke tells us that after his third denial, Jesus turned and looked at Peter. And Peter went out and wept bitterly. Anyone who has ever let a friend or a loved one down badly will know that feeling. Guercino's painting captures Peter's desolating grief at his own perfidy, and it makes one weep just to look at it.

The thing to understand is that Peter didn't know he was going to betray Jesus until he did it. He really did love him. He really did want to die with him. Yet when it came to the test he did the opposite of what he *wanted* to do. It's easy to imagine the desolation he felt after his denials of Jesus. He hated what he had done, and the kind of man it showed him to be. The fact is he didn't know who he was till the moment in the courtyard, when he discovered he was not brave and loyal. He was a weak man, as solid as water. We don't know enough about Peter to understand the factors that destined him to be a betrayer.

The gospels are not biographies. They are sketches. But a skilled cartoonist can reveal a character in a few lines. We get the type instantly, because we are already aware of the complex patterns of human behaviour. There are the boasters hiding from their own fears. There are the haters who despise in others desires they cannot admit in themselves. The contradictions of the self are limitless. And most of what Eliot called our self-lacerations come from our refusal to know ourselves.

Let me draw some conclusions from Peter's story. In the prayer that Jesus taught his disciples, they were to say: 'lead us not into temptation'; or as a modern translation has it: 'let us not be put to the test'. There may have been an element of irony in what Jesus was trying to get them to learn about themselves. He was surrounded by men who boasted they would never forsake him come hell or high water. Yet when the time came, they all ran away. And the loudest boaster and most abject failure was Peter, his right-hand man. Jesus knew how easy it was to go through life untested and therefore ignorant of our own true nature. That's why he warned us not to condemn others for failing tests we had not yet had to face ourselves. That's why the understanding look Jesus gave Peter broke Peter's heart. But it was also the moment Peter began to grow in self-understanding. We can go through life not knowing who we are until the right combination of circumstances puts us to the test and reveals our true character. It's as if our part in the play had been kept from us till the circumstances called it forth and we discovered who we were. But if the moment comes and our character is revealed to us, we must accept it and admit who and what we are.

Once that act of self-acceptance is made, a number of healing acts can follow. The first may go against the grain of everything we have been taught about free will, but it is where we must start. We must acknowledge that our lives were propelled by factors that were never under our control. All the facts of the universe since the curtains lifted on the Big Bang created a script in which we all briefly appeared before leaving the stage to other performers. We are characters in a production that's been running for 14 billion years, and our roles were written for us long before we appeared on the scene. And we don't even know if the show has an author. All of us alive are on stage at the moment, but we'll soon disappear like the 100 billion human beings who preceded us.

> Life's but a walking shadow, a poor player,
> That struts and frets his hour upon the stage,
> And then is heard no more; it is a tale
> Told by an idiot, full of sound and fury,
> Signifying nothing.[29]

The philosopher Mary Warnock tells the same story in a different way. She says that if we lived in laboratory conditions where all the chance elements in our lives from birth could be exactly clocked and recorded, the choices we made as our story unfolded would appear to be foregone conclusions. She says we feel free because we are ignorant of our own genetic system and all the circumstances that programmed the computer that is our own brain. 'Spinoza said that freedom was the ignorance of necessity.'[30] As we shiver at the coldness of this idea, we ought to remind ourselves that it also has a long religious pedigree called Predestination. Religious thinkers trace everything back to God, so it was inevitable that in the compulsions of human behaviour they saw the hand of God. Saint Paul wrestled with the issue in his Letter to the Romans. Like many of us, he was baffled by his own behaviour:

> I do not understand my own actions. For I do not do what I want, but I do the very thing I hate. Now if I do what I do not want, I agree that the law is good. So then it is no longer I that do it, but sin which dwells within me . . . I can will what is right, but I cannot do it. For I do not do the good I want, but the evil I do not want is what I do. Now if I do what I do not want, it is no longer I that do it, but sin which dwells within me.[31]

Paul was a religious visionary not a philosopher, so he found the resolution to the puzzle of his own behaviour in the will of God.

> We know that in everything God works for good with those who love him, who are called according to his purpose. For those whom he foreknew he also predestined . . . And those whom he predestined he also called; and those whom he called he also justified . . . [32]

It's not clear what Paul means here, but the sense is that, however mysteriously, God is directing the show and everything that happens is determined by him. That is certainly how the Protestant Reformer John Calvin understood it. He was in no doubt that

By predestination we mean the eternal decree of God, by which he determined with himself whatever he wished to happen with regard to every man. All are not created on equal terms, but some are preordained to eternal life, others to eternal damnation; and, accordingly, as each has been created for one or other of these ends, we say that he has been predestinated to life or death.[33]

Islam has a similar line. In the Qur'an, Surah 9 tells us: 'Naught shall visit us but what God has prescribed for us.' And it is made even more explicit in one of the reports of Muhammad's table talk known as Hadiths:

There is no one of you, no soul that has been born, but has his place in Paradise or Hell already decreed for him, or to put it otherwise, his unhappy or his happy fate has been decreed for him.[34]

In these quotations, if you substitute for the word 'God' the words 'all the facts of the Universe so far', you are close to Mary Warnock's description of the human situation: in our lives each of us was determined by factors that were beyond our control.

The chances are that you won't like this description of human behaviour in either its religious or its secular version. Like it or not, the facts seem to fit it. As you read these words, two children are born in the same ward of the same hospital. Tomorrow they will be taken home to very different parts of the same city and their predestined stories will unfold, one to success and acclaim, the other to failure and shame. What we need to consider is whether we can alter the script already written for us in any of its versions or whether, as Shakespeare expressed it in Lear: 'As flies to wanton boys are we to the gods', so all we can do is play out the hand dealt to us before shuffling off the stage.[35] There is evidence that another story can be improvised from the script written for us, and I want to introduce it in the words of another philosopher, Hannah Arendt:

> . . . though we don't know what we are doing when we are acting, we have no possibility ever to undo what we have done. Action processes are not only unpredictable, they are also irreversible; there is no author or maker who can undo . . . what he has done if he does not like it or when the consequences are disastrous. The possible redemption from the predicament of irreversibility is the faculty of forgiving . . . Without being forgiven, released from the consequences of what we have done, our capacity to act would . . . be confined to one single deed from which we could never recover; we would remain the victim of its consequences forever.[36]

Our tragedy is that though we do not know what we are doing when we act, our actions are irreversible. There's no rewind button in a human life, though we often wish there were. We long to go back to how things were before we uttered that word or committed that act. But we can't. That's what we said. That's what we did. The tragedy is that our acts go on to determine the behaviour of those they have damaged, and the script drives the action on to the next crisis. Since art imitates life, this is the pattern we see repeated again and again in novels and plays and soap operas. As Jeremiah put it: 'The fathers have eaten sour grapes, and the children's teeth are set on edge.'[37] Arendt suggests that the only way to change the direction of the plot is through forgiveness. Forgiveness cannot reverse the action, but it can reject or interrupt its consequences. Without forgiveness the scripted sequence flows on. And a marriage is destroyed. A career is wrecked. A relationship is shattered.

How does forgiveness happen? Like everything else in human psychology, the ability to forgive seems to be already present or predestined in some but not in others. Nietzsche thought those who were unable to forgive and forget lacked plastic energy:

> In order to determine the extent and thereby the boundary point at which past things must be forgotten if they are not to become the grave diggers of the present, one has to know the exact extent of the plastic energy of a person . . . that is, the power to grow uniquely from within, to transform and incorporate the past and the unknown, to heal wounds, to replace what is lost, and to duplicate shattered structures from within . . . There are people so lacking this energy that they bleed to death, as if from a tiny scratch, after a single incident, a single pain, and often in particular a single minor injustice.[38]

I have known people who fitted this description. Visiting them was to endure a recitation of outrage at an injury from the past, often the distant past. Most of the energy of their life was consumed in rehearsing it. They suffered from a locked-in syndrome that imprisoned them in the memory of the offence. And it played on a loop to those who would listen to it.

If forgiveness is the force that frees victims from this constant playback, what prompts it? An important factor seems to be the spontaneous energy of compassion, the ability to feel or intuit another's distress. In the injured person, compassion for the perpetrators overcomes the pain of the wound they inflicted. In some cases, the compassionate person feels the offenders' distress at their own action. Or the victim feels pity for the one who could do such a thing and be such a person. Wherever it comes from, one of the paradoxes of compassion-forgiveness is that it can release the sorrow of offenders at their own action. This is what happened between Jesus and Peter. Jesus looked with compassion at Peter after his denials, and it caused Peter to weep. Jesus understood the misery Peter felt at discovering he was not the man he thought he was, but the kind of failure he actually turned out to be.

The account of the forgiveness of Peter by Jesus for his denials comes at the end of the Gospel of John. With the tact of the artist, John doesn't *tell* us about Peter's forgiveness, he *shows* it. Jesus is dead, and Peter has gone back to his job as a fisherman on the Sea of Galilee, haunted by his betrayal of the man he loved. Suddenly Jesus is beside him on the beach, but he does not mention the three betrayals. Instead, he asks Peter three times if he loves him. And Peter brings to his three avowals of love the same passion he brought to the denials that had broken his heart.

Peter was not a vicious man: vice is unconscious of

itself. Peter was a weak man: and weakness is all-too conscious of itself. What Jesus gave Peter was the gift to fail without being destroyed by it. This is one of the ways forgiveness works. Peter's threefold renewal of his broken vows could not undo his three denials. His denials were irreversible and could not be undone, but their consequences were halted by forgiveness, and a different script for the future became possible. In Nietzsche's words, the actions of Peter's past were not allowed to become the grave diggers of his future.

In thinking about the mystery of forgiveness and the fact that some seem to forgive with ease and some cannot forgive at all, it is important to get the tone or the mood of our language right. It is not a matter of approving those who can and condemning those who cannot forgive. Even here our natures seem to be predetermined. So it is yet another aspect of human behaviour we should try to understand. If the ability to forgive opens the script in a new direction and offers the possibility of a different future, the inability to forgive does the opposite. It kills and buries the future, and locks the participants not only into the memory of the past but also into all the consequences that will continually flow from it. It reminds me of people I have known who never recovered from the death of a loved one and whose life became a sustained act of mourning. No present, no future, only the compulsive memory of the past. The inability to forgive works the same way. It imprisons us in the past, whether in our personal or in our group relations. That's why most of the wars and feuds that characterise human history are the constant rehearsal of a past offence. In these communities, there is no present, no future, only the compulsive remembrance of the past.

That can be true of individuals as well as of whole communities. They can be trapped in the memory of an offence they committed that has dominated their whole life. They are never able to silence the inner voice that proclaims them a failure. They had their chance and blew it. Moving on from that kind of paralysis requires what for many is the most difficult kind of forgiveness to achieve – self-forgiveness. It is hard to extend compassion to the self for the pain and hurt it has caused others, but there is no worthwhile future without it. The secret lies in the perspective we adopt. We should bring to ourselves the same eyes, the same look, that we brought to those who shared their guilt and sorrow with us. The poet Gerard Manley Hopkins understood that. He was no stranger to self-accusation and depression, so he prayed:

> My own heart let me more have pity on; let
> Me live to my sad self hereafter kind,
> Charitable; not live this tormented mind
> With this tormented mind tormenting yet.[39]

Artists are usually better at expressing the intricacies of the human soul than theologians. Let me prove the point by looking at Edward St Aubyn's series of novels about Patrick Melrose. One way to read them is as an investigation of the dynamics of forgiveness. Patrick is looking back on a life ruined by a father who abused him and a mother who neglected him, a life characterised by destructive addictions and damaged relationships. In the novel

Some Hope, he tries to tell his friend Johnny about the abuse he suffered:

> 'How do you mean 'abused'? asked Johnny uncertainly . . .
>   'I'. . . Patrick couldn't speak. The crumpled bedspread with the blue phoenixes, the pool of cold slime at the base of his spine, scuttling off over the tiles. These were memories he was not prepared to talk about.

He tells Johnny he was sexually abused by his father, adding: 'But now I'm exhausted by hating him. I can't go on.'[40] His predicament is that he can see how his father's abuse had caused the disastrous pattern of his own life:

> He knew that under the tall grass of an apparently untamed future the steel rails of fear and habit were already laid. What he suddenly couldn't bear, with every cell in his body, was to act out the destiny prepared for him by his past, and slide obediently along those rails, contemplating bitterly all the routes he would rather have taken.[41]

A few pages later in the novel, Anne, another friend, asks if he's tried to forgive his father. Patrick replies that to forgive him he'd have to be convinced that his father had made some effort to change the course of his life.

> 'If he'd changed the course he wouldn't need forgiving,' said Anne. 'That's the whole deal with forgiving. Anyhow, I don't say you're not wrong not to forgive him, but you can't stay stuck with this hatred.'[42]

Anne's words perfectly express the human predicament: we may be justified in our refusal to forgive an injury, but it means we are stuck with the hatred we feel for the offender; and the steel rails of our bitterness propel us into the future already scripted for us. It is not till the last page of the final novel in the series, *At Last*, that the resolution is achieved and Patrick is able to tear up the script, forgive and move on:

> . . . he opened himself up to the feeling of utter help-lessness and incoherence that he supposed he had spent his life trying to avoid, and waited for it to dismember him . . . Instead of feeling the helplessness, he felt the helplessness and compassion for the helplessness at the same time. One followed the other swiftly . . . As the compassion expanded he saw himself on equal terms with his supposed persecutors, saw his parents, who appeared to be the cause of his suffering, as unhappy children with parents who appeared to be the cause of their suffering: there was no one to blame and everyone to help, and those who appeared to deserve the most blame needed the most help. For a while he stayed level with the pure inevitability of things being as they were . . . and he saw that there was a margin of freedom . . . in that clarity.[43]

Patrick's 'margin of freedom' was the sudden insight that liberated him from the steel rails of his own past that were forcing him towards a predestined future. Understanding the forces that controlled him gave him enough of a margin of freedom to redirect them. It is only when we acknowledge how imprisoned we are that we become free. This is not far from Spinoza's idea that, although everything is predetermined, our capacity to understand the facts that determine our behaviour gives us a margin of freedom and control over it. Only when we know how bound we are can we break free.

This is a paradox well understood by artists who use their genius to express the human condition. It is there in the myth of the voyage of Odysseus. Odysseus is warned that when he sails past the island of the Sirens, their beautiful voices will lure his ship onto the rocks. So he tells his sailors to plug up their ears and tie him to the mast to prevent them being lured to their own destruction. Understanding his own compulsions gave him a margin of freedom over them. Self-understanding helps us connect our own weaknesses to the weaknesses of others and forgive them. And compassion is the energy that drives it, including compassion for ourselves.

But it can be left too late. That's why the practice of self-examination is worth mastering early in life, while there may still be time to rewrite the script and make a happier story. Not that it's ever entirely in our own hands. I've known men – they have usually been men – who have died consumed with regret because their mistakes were not met with forgiveness at the time, and the steel rails running out of their past drove them away from those they loved. One of them was consumed with sorrow that he was dying without ever having met his grandchildren. An affair had broken his marriage and provoked an enduring bitterness in his wife, who made sure he lost his family when he injured her. And of course she lost everything as well, because her life had become an act of revenge against him. The price of her inability to forgive was imprisonment in the kind of hatred Patrick Melrose had finally managed to escape from. What harm we can unknowingly do to each other! Our own hearts let us more have pity on.

Bringing all this together at the end of a long and muddled life can be painful, especially if we are trying to do it on our own. This is where religious traditions can help us even if we are not religious. Making a confession or owning up can be a beautiful and releasing act as we face the end of life. And we can do it in any number of ways. We can confess to a priest if that's our style; or to a friend, if we need a listening ear. But the pillow on our bed or the flowers at the bottom of the garden will do just as well. It's only a matter of being honest, with the right mixture of compassion. Yes, that's who I was, we can say with a sigh. That's what I did. Wish I hadn't, but it's too late now. Forgive me.

Then we should let it go. The last bus is on its way . . .

IV

THEN WHAT?

What will it be like, our last moment alive? The chances are that we won't be alert enough to notice it. Our doctors will try to make it as easy as possible, so we may not be conscious when we finally slip away. But suppose we are. Suppose we are aware till the very end, will we notice it? Will we know it is the final moment? Will there be any sense of pulling up anchor and casting off? There is an old poetic tradition that imagines death as a sea journey. In Greek mythology, everyone had to pay Charon the ferryman in order to cross the river Styx, the boundary between the worlds of the living and the dead. Other poets have used the same metaphor. To describe the moment of death, Tennyson used the image of crossing the sandbar to catch the tide where the river meets the sea:

> . . . such a tide as moving seems asleep,
> Too full for sound and foam,
> When that which drew from out the boundless deep
> Turns again home.[44]

Is this pure artistry or is there some collective memory in humanity that poets draw on when thinking about death?

The poet Michael Donaghy used the analogy of the car-ferry to anticipate his own early death, as if he were standing on the passenger deck of his own body looking down on 'the skilled frenzy' of the workers on the pier as they released the mooring ropes and sent him out to sea:

> You will do the very last thing.
> Wait then for a noise in the chest,
> between depth charge and gong,
> like the seadoors slamming on the car deck.
> Wait for the white noise and then cold astern.
>
> Gaze down over the rim of the enormous lamp.
> Observe the skilled frenzy of the physicians,
> a nurse's bald patch, blood. These will blur,
> as sure as you've forgotten the voices
> of your childhood friends, or your toys.
>
> Or, you may note with mild surprise,
> your name. For the face they now cover
> is a stranger's and it always has been.
> Turn away. We commend you to the light,
> Where all reliable accounts conclude.[45]

When death finally arrives, will we see it coming or watch ourselves leaving or casting off? Is it possible to imagine what that might feel like and what our reaction might be? Maybe because I am writing this book and thinking about death constantly, I had a dream recently in which I knew that my moment had come. It was a standard falling dream, according to Freud one of the most common and universal types. They are usually described as *fear*-of-falling-dreams, and analysts have offered many interpretations of their meaning. The fact that they are as common as they are suggests that they carry a straightforward anxiety about stumbling off a great height. I've known people who suffered from vertigo and could not walk up a hill as unthreatening as Arthur's Seat in Edinburgh without having to summon colossal resources of courage. I don't have that fear, but I have felt its opposite. I have looked down from a high cliff and wondered what it would feel like to throw myself off or let myself drop. There is obviously something in dreams of falling that expresses either a brute fear of, or a dangerous attraction to, losing control of our bodies and their purchase on reality. It is only a short step to a more psychological interpretation in which falling is not about losing physical traction but about losing safety or purpose or meaning in our lives.

Inevitably, experts offer us their interpretation of these cloudy experiences. I have no desire to join the queue of interpreters. And I know that other people's dreams are the archetype of tedium. So I'll be brief about my dream. As I was having it, I knew that it was not about the fear of falling. It was about the experience of dying. I was drifting into empty space like an astronaut separated from a satellite. I remember the strange weightlessness, the sense of having nothing to hold on to any more. The dominant feeling was of resigned curiosity. So this is what it feels like to be dying, I said to myself as I floated away. Then I woke up. The experience was of dying not of being dead. Being dead is beyond or past all experience. But dying isn't. It is something we can take part in, be aware of. I hope I am alert when it happens so that I can greet it and in some sense own it or choose it.

The novelist Henry James is said to have recognised it when it came for him. 'So here it is at last, the distinguished thing,' he exclaimed. That suggests that though we might recognise death's *approach* – whether as a tide we catch or as a bus drawing to a halt at our stop or a falling into space – it is hard to imagine what the moment of leaving will actually feel like, the event of death itself. Until recently no one came back to tell us, but with the successes of modern medicine that has changed. Now we have the testimony of many people who claim to have 'died' and been restored to life by their doctors. They even have an acronym to identify themselves: NDEs, people who have had 'near-death-experiences' or, in the shorthand of the movement, 'experiencers'. And a movement they have certainly become. Millions of copies of books have been sold that describe and draw metaphysical conclusions from people who have 'died' and been brought back to life. So what do they tell us?

Most of them recount experiences of pleasure and acceptance. A common claim is that their souls were released from their bodies and hovered over them in the hospital room, watching what the poet Michael Donaghy described as 'the skilled frenzy of the physicians' working hard to defibrillate or resuscitate them. Others claim to have gone through brightly lighted tunnels into a world where they were welcomed by angelic figures and dead members of their own families. 'Experiencers' come back from these encounters changed for the better and convinced they are proof of the existence of the soul, an immortal entity that is related to but is independent of the body and goes on to another life when the body packs in. But not all near-death-experiences are pleasant. About twenty-three per cent of those reported are described as distressing. They tell of finding themselves in an ugly and foreboding landscape where the soul, though not being actively punished, experiences a desolating void.

***

Sceptical scientists do not deny these near-death-experiences in either their positive or negative forms. But they offer naturalistic or materialistic explanations for them. They think they do not so much prove the existence of the soul as reflect a previously held belief in its existence, which is then used to interpret what occurred. Sceptics offer a different explanation. They describe NDEs as hallucinations – events in the human mind with no reality outside it – induced by oxygen shortage, a common result of cardiac arrest. The experiencers were not actually floating outside themselves, but the neural connections that linked them to their own bodies had shut down and induced a feeling of separation. And it is well known that drugs can produce the same effect.

I remember visiting a parishioner in Edinburgh's old Royal Infirmary late one winter afternoon. He had suffered heart problems for years and was being treated for yet another attack. When I arrived at his bedside in the huge ward, he indicated that he wanted me to pull the screens round the bed so they couldn't hear us talking. Then he whispered to me that at three o'clock that morning his doctors and nurses had taken him to the Forth Bridge and suspended him over the dark waters below, where for hours he hung terrified. And he knew they were planning another excursion for him tonight. I told him not to be afraid, I'd deal with it. On my way out, I spoke to the ward sister. 'It'll be that new drug he's on,' she said. 'We'll change it.' They did, and the hallucinations ceased; but not before they'd scared him almost to death.

If this proves nothing else, it reminds us that the human mind is a mysterious, shifting continent, and we have only just begun to explore it. The mind is its own place and does its own thing. In our time, it is being investigated by psychologists and neuroscientists, but artists have always been its best explorers. The poet John Milton said the mind could make a hell of heaven or a heaven of hell. The poet Gerard Manley Hopkins knew how frightening it could be:

> O the mind, mind has mountains, cliffs of fall
> Frightful, sheer, no-man-fathomed. Hold them cheap
> May who ne'er hung there.[46]

For as far back as we can trace our own story, death has been one of the mind's obsessions. And it seems to be unique to us. So obsessed are we with the knowledge of our mortality that Martin Heidegger, one of the great philosophers of the twentieth century, defined the human animal as a 'Being-toward-Death', one who was always old enough to die – and knew it.[47] He described our condition as 'thrownness', finding ourselves thrust or thrown into a life we neither asked for nor understand the meaning of

– yet with the knowledge that one day, maybe one day soon, it would be taken from us. On earth – maybe even in the whole universe – this knowledge seems to be unique to us. Of course it is impossible for us to fathom the inner or spiritual lives of the other creatures we share the world with, but they do not seem to live with the constant knowledge that one day they'll die. In a chorus from his play *The Dog Beneath the Skin*, W.H. Auden meditates on the unselfconscious immediacy of the animal's life.

Happy the hare at morning, for she cannot read
The hunter's waking thoughts. Lucky the leaf
Unable to predict the fall . . .
. . . the mineral stars disintegrating quietly into light.
But what shall man do, who can whistle tunes by heart,
Know to the bar when death shall cut him short,
   like the cry of the shearwater?[48]

All animals fight death when it threatens, like Leonard Woolf's blind puppies. And there is evidence that some of them grieve the death of their fellows. But most of them seem to move on and forget what happened. They certainly don't care for their dead the way we do. They let them disintegrate where they drop, whereas we give our dead funerals and erect memorials to them and go on wondering what has happened to them. In fact, it would be little exaggeration to say that it was the fate of the dead that started us thinking. Thinking about ourselves and the world in which we found ourselves. Much came from that thinking, including religion, which is best understood as belief in spheres of reality behind or beyond, but related to the one we inhabit while we are alive. And looking at the dead and wondering what happened to them might have been what got it going.

The most obvious thing they noticed about the dead was that something that used to happen in them had stopped happening. They no longer breathed. It was a small step to associate the act of breathing with the idea of something dwelling within, yet separate from, the physical body that gave it life. The Greeks called it *psyche,* the Romans *spiritus,* both from verbs meaning to breathe or blow. A spirit or soul was what made a body live and breathe. It inhabited the body for a time. And when the body died, it departed. But where did it go? One explanation was that it had gone somewhere else, the way a person could inhabit a place for a time then move out. This *somewhere else* grew into the idea of a spiritual world on the flipside of the physical one we inhabit while we are alive on earth.

Though our distant ancestors left only silent traces of their thinking, from about 130,000 BCE onwards we have discovered evidence that may point to a belief in life after death. Food, tools and ornaments were placed in graves, suggesting that the dead were thought to have travelled on into some kind of afterlife and needed to be equipped for the journey. Another practice was the painting of the bodies of the dead with red ochre, maybe to symbolise blood and the idea of continuing life. This was found in one of the oldest known burials, of a mother and child at Qafzeh in Israel from around 100,000 BCE. The same practice is found in Australia in 42,000 BCE at Lake Mango, where the body was also covered in red ochre. By 10,000 BCE, we have evidence that burial rites were not only more elaborate but in some places they had also become ferociously cruel, with the execution of wives and servants as part of the funeral ceremony. The slaughter of the widows of important men has been widely practised in different cultures, though whether to maintain the comfort and status of the VIP in the life that awaited him after death or as a way of appeasing or buying off the spirits of the dead, we cannot say for certain.

And marking where the dead lay became important, especially if they were significant figures. Sometimes they were laid under gigantic boulders, sometimes in carefully constructed stone chambers called dolmens, which consisted of two upright stones supporting a large lid. It has been suggested that piling boulders over the graves of the dead might have been designed to keep them underground where they belonged, so that they wouldn't start wandering the earth as ghosts. Even now there are people who are reluctant to walk through a graveyard alone on a dark night for fear of what they might encounter, proof that ancient anxieties about the state of the dead still persist. An old fear is that some of the dead are either unable to accept or are unaware of the fact that they are dead, so they can't move on and hang around to haunt the living. A practising psychic I knew once told me that after 1945 he had been used by a department of the War Office to settle the unquiet spirits of soldiers whose bodies had been obliterated by bombs that had left no physical trace of their existence.

There's an enormous literature about the existence of these displaced entities. We call them ghosts, the Old

English word for spirits, disembodied souls who hang around their old neighbourhoods. Most priests have been called upon to try to deal with the presence of unsettled spirits haunting a house and distressing the living. I have been called upon several times in this way and have always responded positively. At the time, I was more open to the possibility of the supernatural than I am now, but even then I was never sure whether I was ministering to the living or the dead. But what I did always seemed to settle the disturbance. Maybe it was another example of the usefulness of Negative Capability in responding to human need. It was the act itself not how I understood it that mattered.

On one occasion I was phoned by the warden of a university hall of residence at the top of the Royal Mile in Edinburgh. A group of students had been fooling around with a Ouija board when the room suddenly became icy cold and they were spooked by a sense of presence. Ouija boards – from the French word for 'yes' – are flat slabs with letters, numbers, symbols and the words 'yes', 'no' and 'goodbye' on them. Participants place their fingers on a heart-shaped piece of wood or plastic called a planchette. Guided or prompted by the dead who are trying to get in touch, the planchette moves around the board spelling out words and messages for the living. Sceptics say the planchette's movement is achieved by the body's own reflexes, what they call the ideomotor effect, a bit like the naturalistic explanation of NDEs as hallucinations. As with a lot of the weird stuff that happens to us, they say it's all in the mind. But we've already registered that the human mind has a disconcerting power that's all its own. It has even been claimed that those who have survived near-death experiences have an effect on electrical equipment. It is reported that at one conference of Near Death Experiencers the hotel's computer system went down.[49] So it's not hard to believe that if the mind can interfere with a computer's software, it could much more easily mess with a body's temperature levels. However you explain what happens in a Ouija board session, the effects can be spooky and scary, as they were that Sunday night in an old building up near Edinburgh Castle. I prayed with the students, the atmosphere shifted and calm was restored.

On another occasion, I was asked by the owner of an ancient castle south of Edinburgh, which he ran as a hotel, if I could help him. Some of his cleaners had refused to work in a room in the castle because of its unearthly coldness and sense of oppressive despair. His research had suggested that centuries ago children had been murdered in that room. He didn't know what to believe, except that it was damaging his business and upsetting his staff. Could I help? Again, I prayed with the owner and his staff, and whatever the disturbance was or wherever it was happening – in the room or in the minds of the cleaners – the situation was calmed.

However we interpret or explain these experiences, in them we catch a glimpse of belief in another world or another life beyond this one, which is connected to it, with death as the gateway between them. But let me leave ghosts to their wanderings on this side of death and ask a different question. Is anything waiting for *us* on the *other side*? Whether we actually experience what is happening to us when we die, whether we are conscious of the ferry pulling out from the shore or the bus moving away from the kerb, the big question is whether it is taking us anywhere. We die. Then what? What happens next? Very different answers have been given to that question. I'll begin with the most complicated, which comes from India and the oldest of the organised religions, Hinduism.[50]

According to Hindu teaching, your soul or spirit is a wanderer that's had many lives in the past before it came into the one you happen to be in at the moment. And it will live many more lives in the future when this one is over. The technical term for this belief is reincarnation or metempsychosis, and it is an intricate version of the doctrine of predestination we thought about in the previous chapter. Each of your lives will be determined by how you acted in the one before this, just as how you are behaving now will influence the kind of life you'll have on the next turn of the wheel. This is called the doctrine of '*karma*' or 'the law of the deed': actions have consequences. When the thinkers of India looked at the dead and wondered where they had gone, this was the idea they came up with. Souls did not die, either in the sense that they ceased altogether or in the sense that they travelled on into another sphere of permanent existence beyond death. The Hindu mind believed that the soul came back to earth again in another body, whose status was dictated by its karma.

Existence was a colossal recycling process in which the quality of the life that went through the door marked 'death' affected the status of what emerged through the door on the other side marked 'rebirth'. They called the system '*samsara*' or 'wandering-through', because souls were carried through it to their next shape and the next and the one after that, far into the disappearing future. For good or ill, every action the soul committed in its current life affected the quality of its next appearance. But they did not think of karma as a punishment devised by a heavenly judge. It was an impersonal law like gravity, in which one thing followed another as effect followed cause.

In its wanderings, the soul might go through millions of lives before achieving escape into a state called *nirvāna,* from a word meaning to be blown out like a candle. How to escape from the wheel of existence and be blown into nothingness was the ultimate purpose of Hindu religion. It is interesting that at its centre is the idea that existence can become a burden and failure to die a torment. Here it reflects another of the mind's obsessions that has also been well rehearsed by poets. A Greek myth captures the sorrow of it. The myth concerns a beautiful Trojan called Tithonus who asked the Goddess Aurora for immortality. But he forgot to ask for eternal youth and vigour, so he grew old and weak but could never die. His predicament was captured by the English poet Alfred, Lord Tennyson.

> The woods decay, the woods decay and fall,
> The vapours weep their burthen to the ground,
> Man comes and tills the field and lies beneath,
> And after many summers dies the swan.
> Me only cruel immortality
> Consumes: I wither slowly in thine arms . . .
> A white-haired shadow roaming like a dream
> The ever-silent spaces of the East . . . [51]

Imagine what that would be like. Actually, it doesn't take much imagination, because the karma of modern medicine keeps too many people alive long after any pleasure or meaning has gone from their lives. Sentenced to years of mournful disso-lution, many of them long to be blown out like a candle.

Sceptics are usually too quick to reject the narratives of religion, especially if they believe them to be as unlikely as the multiple elaborations of Hinduism. They fail to realise that they are one of the ways in which the human mind gives form to its fears and anxieties. That's why the ideas of karma and samsara can carry meaning for people who continue to take them seriously long after they have ceased to take them literally. And it's why the word karma has become shorthand for understanding important aspects of human behaviour. Our acts have consequences not only for ourselves but for others. And they can rever-berate down the ages. Because our fathers ate sour grapes yesterday, our teeth are set on edge today.

The soul's wandering through samsara may be a weari-some prospect, but the alternative offered by the other two big religions in the world is, if anything, even more depressing. Hinduism promises an ultimate escape from existence after many false starts. However long it takes, one day our candle will be blown out because, in Hinduism, God or ultimate reality is infinitely patient. In the words of the poet A.S.J. Tessimond:

> He gives you time in heaven to do as you please,
> To climb love's gradual ladder by slow degrees
> Gently to rise from sense to soul, to ascend
> To a world of timeless joy, world without end.[52]

That's not how it goes in Christianity and Islam. According to these religious systems, the human soul is a one-shot deal that is heavy with eternal consequences. What we make of ourselves in the single life we get on earth determines where and how we'll spend it in the next. We don't get to come back again and again till we finally achieve a pass and go on to the University of Nirvana. Our one life is an examination in which no re-sits are permitted. Heaven is the name of the destination for those who pass; hell for those who fail.

Though it takes their existence for granted, Christianity's scripture, the New Testament, is sparing in its descriptions of heaven and hell, a reserve that was more than compensated for by later preachers and theologians, as we'll see. Where the New Testament was reticent, the Qur'an was clear from the beginning. It contains a number of chapters or '*surahs*' in which heaven and hell are described. The most famous is Surah 56, On the Day of Judgement. Heaven or paradise is a Garden of Delight that might have been designed for the exclusive enjoyment of the male of the human species. As a reward for their sufferings on earth, there are springs of wine on tap that don't intoxicate or cause a hangover, and beautiful, wide-eyed young women are available for their enjoyment. That's what's prepared for those the Qur'an calls Companions of the Right, the good. It's a very different deal for those it calls the Companions of the Left, the wicked. It's hell for them, 'mid burning winds and boiling waters and the shadow of a smoking blaze . . .'[53]

In both Christianity and Islam, just as heaven is a place of unending joy so is hell a place of unending torment.

Hell is pain without any hope of respite or release. It is a furnace that never fails. Here's a description of its chemistry from a sermon the Irish writer James Joyce heard when he was a schoolboy:

> . . . the sulphurous brimstone which burns in hell is a substance which is specially designed to burn for ever and for ever with unspeakable fury. Moreover, our earthly fire destroys at the same time as it burns, so that the more intense it is the shorter is its duration; but the fire of hell has this property, that it preserves that which it burns, and, though it rages with incredible intensity, it rages for ever.[54]

Saint Thomas Aquinas, the Catholic Church's greatest theologian, claimed that one of the attractions of heaven was that it had a convenient balcony from which its citizens could watch the torments of the damned down below: 'The blessed in the kingdom of heaven will see the punishments of the damned, so that their bliss will be that much greater.'[55] But Aquinas was also the theologian who offered a way to avoid hell with the invention of purgatory, the spiritual laundry system we thought about in Chapter One. This is an example of how the more thoughtful religions have been good at finding ways to soften their own doctrinal excesses. There have even been Christian theologians who believed that while hell existed in theory, in practice it had never acquired any inhabitants.

It is worth noting here that those who invented these post-mortem destinations were never in agreement about the timings involved in the transitions between them. Some

gave the impression that at death the transfer was imme-
diate. One moment you were alive in this world. You died,
and the next moment you faced the judge who would
immediately determine your forthcoming destination –
hell, purgatory or heaven. This is still the official position
of the Roman Catholic Church. It teaches that just as the
soul was created at the instant of conception so at the
instant of death it immediately faces judgement. This is
why it continues to warn the faithful against dying uncon-
fessed and unprepared.

There is an older tradition that saw judgement not as
an individual but as a group process. All the world's dead
would hibernate in their graves until the Day of Judgement.
The Last Trumpet would sound, their atoms would reas-
semble into resurrected bodies, and they would stand to
hear their fate. The belief that the bodies as well as the
souls of the dead would rise from their graves to be
judged on the Last Day had a profound effect on Christian
burial customs. Cremation was a problem because it made
the re-assembling of the body hard to imagine. That was
why in the Roman Empire, under the influence of
Christianity, by the fifth century cremation had been abandoned. It was not revived in the West till the nineteenth
century. Even then it took Christian churches a long time
to accept it. The Roman Catholic Church did not permit
its use till 1963. Uneasiness about it persists, reflected in
a Vatican decree in 2016 forbidding Catholics from
keeping the ashes of their departed at home, scattering
them in nature or dividing them between members of the
family. Ashes are only to be kept in holy places such as
churches or cemeteries.

If you are confident in your religious faith, these incon-
sistencies may not trouble you, but what are those of us
who can't take them literally to make of them? A good
way to think about religion is as a Rorschach test that maps
humanity's psychic geography. It reveals us to ourselves.
So the question is whether religion causes or just expresses
and gives form to our obsession with death. The answer
seems to be a bit of both. Religion emphasises our fear
of death in order to assuage it. It frightens in order to
save. Because it takes death very seriously and thinks we
should as well. Catholicism has been pastorally more skilful
at managing these complexities than the severer versions
of Protestantism. Catholicism's descriptions of hell were
terrifying, but they were always followed by helpful directions on how to avoid it. And the reassurance of their
Last Rites took a lot of the anguish out of dying. That's
why Catholic Army Chaplains were thought to be more
effective than Protestants in ministering to dying soldiers
in No Man's Land in the First World War. They had a rite,
a formal mechanism of mercy and forgiveness that reas-
sured the dying in their last moments in terrible
circumstances. I have ministered these rites myself and
seen the peace they can bring at the end. I have sent good
friends into the arms of a merciful God I was no longer
sure I believed in. And I was convinced not only of the
efficacy but of the honesty of what I was doing. I was
not there to ventilate my doubts but to help the dying find
the strength to cast off and take the tide that was pulling
them out.

I have also been helpless to assuage the fear of a dying
friend because the dread that paralysed him allowed me

no way to console him. Brought up in a strict Calvinist sect, on his death bed he reverted to the Predestinarianism he had been schooled in as a child. God, he had been taught, predestined some to heaven and some to hell, not for any good or ill they had done but simply according to his mysterious will. How could he be certain what God intended for him, heaven or hell? I tried to batter through the fear that gripped him to open him to the loving God of the parables of Jesus, but he died in fear not in hope.

Whatever we make of the different responses of religion to death and what may follow, they show that from the beginning death has obsessed humanity. It continues to obsess us. It is what the theologian Paul Tillich called an 'ultimate concern'. It comes with being human. We can't help wondering about it. But in our day it is no longer just religion that offers us a way to transcend death and achieve everlasting life. Modern science has now entered the game. But there's a big difference between its approach and religion's. It is no longer God who offers us eternal life; it is science-based technology. And when it comes, it won't be lived in heaven. It will happen right here on earth. The plan is to conquer or outrun death so completely that we'll postpone it indefinitely. It will be immortality on the instalment plan. The scientists who are working on it tell us they are not there yet, but they're speeding along nicely. Meanwhile, for those of us unfortunate enough to die before death has been finally conquered, the best bet is to have our corpses preserved by freezing them – cryo-preserved in the jargon – so that science can resurrect them when it has perfected the technology. It is reminiscent of religious eschatology, but without the supernatural element. The last trump won't be blown by the Archangel Gabriel. A guy in a white coat will do it. It will be a secular salvation, the only one that'll work, according to its evangelists, because we are alone in the universe, and if we want to live forever we'll have to see to it ourselves.

So what will they do to us if we sign on for this eternal life plan? And where do we go to get it done? There are four companies that offer the service, three in the United States and one in Russia. The largest is the Alcor Life Extension Foundation near Phoenix in Arizona. Alcor offers two procedures to customers who have signed up for its version of eternal life. In the basic procedure, which costs $200,000, Alcor's technicians drain the blood from the corpse – 'patient' in their lexicon – and replace it with anti-freeze and other organ-preserving chemicals. It is then lowered head first into a tank or flask filled with liquid nitrogen where it is preserved at a temperature of minus 190 Centigrade. There it will rest until secular resurrection day when it will be thawed and re-animated to emerge blinking into the world of whatever century it happens to be at the time. There's a cheaper option at $80,000 called 'neuro-only', in which the head alone is preserved. The deal here is that on cryo-resurrection day the brain and the mind it carries will be digitally scanned, purged of any unnecessary neuro-junk, and the good stuff left will be uploaded onto an artificial body or robotic prosthesis where it will exist for ever unimpeded by the ills that mortal flesh is heir to.[56]

It is reckoned that hundreds of people have already

availed themselves of the opportunity and hang suspended in cold storage, waiting for resurrection day, some of them having taken their pets along with them for the ride. And it is reported that several thousand people still alive have signed up for the process and paid their deposit. Doubtless, cryo-preservation will soon be an option in private health insurance plans, but it may not be the way to go in the long run. Better than dying and being cryo-preserved till resurrection day would be not to die at all or to live so long that you'd hardly know the difference. That's what the Founder and Director of Alcor is betting on. In a conversation with the writer Mark O'Connell, he explained it like this:

> 'I'm hoping to avoid having to be preserved. My ideal scenario is I stay healthy and take care of myself, and more funding goes into life-extension research, and we actually achieve longevity escape velocity.' He was referring here to the scenario projected by the life-extension impresario Aubrey de Grey, a scientific advisor to Alcor, whereby for every year that passes, the process of longevity research is such that average human life expectancy increases by more than a year – a situation that would, in theory, lead to our effectively outrunning death.[57]

Many scientists doubt the effectiveness of the processes on offer and believe that the brain will be irreversibly damaged by the anti-freeze pumped into it. And they think it highly unlikely that we will achieve enough 'longevity escape velocity' to outrun death forever. But it's not the science that bothers me. Clever humans are constantly breaking the sound barrier of what's achievable. So who is to say that bringing the frozen dead back to life will never happen? Or extracting the human mind from its perishable container of flesh and uploading it onto an imperishable machine? Or outrunning death so effectively that the CEO of Alcor will get the thousand years he desires? It's what comes next that worries me. We are a clever and revolutionary species, and we have spent our history achieving the impossible. But we have been bad at anticipating the effect of our inventiveness, not only on our own health and happiness but also on the health of the planet that is – still – our only viable home. So it's worth giving the anti-death movement some thought.

We should certainly be concerned about the cryopreserved individuals who will emerge blinking into the light of a world that may be beyond their comprehension and for which they will be totally unprepared. I suppose it is possible that a government of the future might organise some kind of reception process for these refugees from the past. They might cluster them together in communities of the ex-dead, because who else could possibly understand their situation? But I wouldn't bet on their getting a generous reception from the not-yet-dead section of the population. Humanity has a bad record when it comes to welcoming strangers, especially if they are considered strange or different. And strange these returnees from death will certainly be. If it works, the problems will soon pile up.

How many cryonic cycles will be permitted for each

individual? Will people keep dying and coming back? And what about the poor, how are they going to respond to yet another privilege only the wealthy will be able to afford? The process is expensive, so the poor will have to stay dead when they die or opt for an inferior resurrection deal, stoking rebellion at yet another form of discrimination. Traditional forms of discrimination based on race, gender, class and wealth are dangerous and unhealthy for humanity, but at least they are finite. Death cancels them. In the grave all are equal. But if even the grave can be bought off, in the future we will have created the ultimate form of inequality. And we already know from our history how inequality promotes violence and revolt. The more daring and angry among the poor will organise themselves into protest movements to raid the cryonic-storage facilities and drain the privileged dead of their anti-freeze. They are also likely to turn their violence on the new strangers in their midst, the cryonically resurrected. As well as becoming victims of social tumult, the ex-dead will almost certainly suffer from psychological problems that will present the psychiatric community with yet another intractable human sorrow. Suicides will become epidemic amongst them, the ultimate irony: death as the friend of the ex-dead.

But the danger will go far beyond the pain of individuals and communities. Suppose we muddle towards some sort of resolution of the problems the ex-dead will create for society. Suppose we slowly come to an accommodation with the reality of regiments of the ex-dead returning to life in our midst either in their old bodies or transplanted into machines. We will have succeeded in fashioning a global boa constrictor that will slowly squeeze us all to death. Our already depleted planet will find it impossible to sustain an exponentially growing population of humans. And while the rest of humanity suffocates, the wealthy will gate themselves into fortified enclaves while they prepare rockets to get them off earth onto palatial space satellites from which they'll watch the disintegration of our once-hospitable blue planet – all because of our denial of death.

I have delivered an apocalyptic scenario here, but it is mirrored in many of the dystopian fictions of our time, artists being our most reliable futurists. That's why it is worth contemplating where our denial of death might yet take us. The American theologian Reinhold Niebuhr wrote a prayer that was intended to instil a sense of realism in the way we manage human affairs. *God, grant us the courage to change what can be changed; the serenity to accept what cannot be changed; and the wisdom to know the difference.* A new clause might be added to the prayer to give it more relevance to the theme of this book: *God, keep us from the folly of interfering too much with the imperatives and contingencies of nature.* We are a clever but not always a wise species, so our battle not only to delay death but to reverse it may turn out to be the greatest folly in the long record of folly that is human history. If we refuse the paradox that it is through death that life is constantly renewed, we may end in the paradox that our denial of death has made life unbearable. It will take all our wisdom to help us navigate the difference.

***

Thinking about these rival eschatologies, the secular and the supernatural, the scientific or the religious, makes me wonder what it is that prompts us to want eternal life in either form. Is it a kind of fear? Not wanting to die too soon or before I am ready to leave the party I can understand, but to *fear* leaving it? What's that about? I can understand the fear of death that religion might induce, given its descriptions of what might happen next. But why would unbelievers who reject any idea of an afterlife also fear death? And we know they do. We know that fear of death is an entirely ecumenical emotion. It is found in unbelievers as well as believers. The novelist Julian Barnes is one of them. He is an unbeliever who fears death and has written about it. Here's what he says in his book, *Nothing to be Frightened Of*:

> Perhaps the important divide is less between the religious and the irreligious as between those who fear death and those who don't. We fall thereby into four categories, and it's clear which two regard themselves as superior: those who do not fear death because they have faith, and those who do not fear death despite having no faith. These groups take the moral high ground. In third place come those who, despite having faith, cannot rid themselves of the old, visceral, rational fear. And then, out of the medals, below the salt, up shit creek, come those of us who fear death and have no faith.[58]

What is it that prompts what Barnes calls the 'old, visceral, rational fear' of death? What is he afraid *of*? If what awaits us after death is not samsara and its endless wandering through other lives; if it is not hell and its endless torment; if it is not even heaven and its endless joy; if it is no-thing, no-where, no-anything, why fear it? Sadness at leaving: of course. Wistfulness at missing the future, particularly the future of those we love: of course. But fear – of nothing?

If we are fortunate enough not to have that fear, maybe we should listen to Julian Barnes again. For him the fear of death is just *there*. It is intrinsic to death. Death carries it, comes with it. *Timor mortis conturbat me,* as an old litany has it. The fear of death disturbs me, *deranges* me. Even though there's nothing on the other side of it; even though death is the end, the full stop, the absolute cessation; the very thought of it scares us. It is as if because being and the matter that clothed it once exploded into existence out of nothing, it now carries within itself the dread of returning to the void from which it escaped. Being dreads Un-being. It is the instinctive reflex of the little blind puppy again.

But why doesn't it scare all of us? Is our hold on life less strong? I belong to one of the two categories Julian Barnes accuses of feeling superior because they do not fear death. The prospect of death saddens but does not frighten me, though I neither desire nor expect life after death. But it doesn't make me feel superior. People play the hand they are dealt in life. I was dealt several cards marked THINGS TO BE AFRAID OF, but NOTHINGNESS was not one of them. Of course, I cannot be certain that as I feel it approaching I won't experience the 'old, visceral, rational fear' of death Barnes describes. After all, I have seen it happen to others. But if it does hit me, I hope I'll be brave enough to endure it. If I lie in fear on my deathbed, I hope someone will say to me: Courage! There are times when we just have to summon the courage to take what's coming. As Shakespeare put it in *King Lear*, we have to endure our going hence even as our coming hither.[59]

If courage is the wise person's response to the fear of going, what is the wise person's answer to those who insist on staying and lust for yet more life, either here on earth in a secular eternity or there in heaven in the supernatural version? In a word, it is gratitude. The opposite of gratitude for life is greed for more of it. It is the inability to enjoy what we have now because we are already lusting after the next edition. The Buddha was right: craving is our curse, the desire for more our scourge. It has made us unhappy, as well as ungrateful, and it might soon make our planet uninhabitable. So be brave in the face of death; be sad at leaving. But don't let those be your final emotions. Let it be gratitude for the life you had. And even if you think there's no one there to hear you, say 'Thank you'. That's what the best poets do. And if you can't find the words yourself, read them instead. Here's how Clive James does it . . .

A pause to grieve,
Burned by the starlight of our lives laid bare,
And then no sound, no sight, no thought. Nowhere.

What is it worth, then, this insane last phase
When everything about you goes downhill?

This much: you get to see the cosmic blaze
And feel its grandeur, even against your will,
As it reminds you, just by being there,
That it is here we live or else nowhere.[60]

V

DEFYING DEATH

My father was born in 1904, and at the end of the Great War, when he was fourteen, he started serving his time as an apprentice block printer at the famous United Turkey Red Factory on the banks of the river Leven in Alexandria. Block printers were the elite of the textile factories that ran along that swift-flowing river. They even had the right to wear bowler hats to work, as a symbol of their status at the top of the journeyman tree. But while he was still a young man, changes in technology rendered his trade obsolete, and for the rest of his life he had to settle for any work he could get. He carried coal for years, but when the Second World War started he was re-employed by the United Turkey Red, dyeing cloth. And when they made him redundant again aged sixty, he ended his working days as a porter in the Vale of Leven Hospital.

He was the kind of man who endured hardship without complaining, but I often wondered how he felt about the way his life had played out. One day I discovered a clue. We lived in a classic Scottish two-roomed cottage known as a room and kitchen, with a recess in the kitchen for a bed. I was rummaging under the bed there when I came across a heavy bundle wrapped in old cloth. I pulled it out and found two heavy lead mallets with short wooden handles. They were your father's mells when he was a tradesman, my mother told me, for the block printing. I was a heedless child, but something about those symbols of his former status quietened and saddened me. Why had he kept them? A sense of betrayal and disappointment clung to them. Time and change have always robbed the poor of their occupations, and of the pride and purpose they gave them. In human history, the buffeting of the poor seems to operate like a law as impersonal as karma. As befits a clever, revolutionary species who can't leave anything alone for long, we are constantly inventing new ways of doing things; and just as constantly discarding those who had mastered the old ways, like my father with his treasured mells.

This is a theme deeply embedded in Scottish literature, the sorrow of it caught by our best writers. At the end of Scotland's favourite novel, Lewis Grassic Gibbon's *Sunset Song*, the people of Kinraddie go up Blawearie Brae to dedicate the Memorial to the four men of the town who fell in the Great War. And the minister preaches a short, powerful sermon.

With them we may say there died a thing older than themselves – these were the Last of the Peasants, the last of the Old Scots folk. A new generation comes up that will know them not, except as a memory in a song . . .

The last of the peasants – those four that you knew – took that with them to the darkness and the quietness of the places where they sleep. And the land

changes – their parks and their steadings are a desolation where the sheep are pastured – we are told that
great machines come soon to till the land, and the
great herds come to feed on it – the crofter has gone,
the man with the house and the steading of his own
and the land closer to his heart than the flesh of his
own body. Nothing, it has been said, is true but change,
nothing abides . . . [61]

Nothing is true but change, nothing abides. And I think of that
sad wee bundle under the bed in Random Street, Alexandria.

In *Cloud Howe*, the second volume in Gibbon's trilogy,
we hear his main character Chris meditating on time and
the change it brings:

In a ten years' time what things might have been? She
might stand on this hill, she might rot in a grave, it
would matter nothing, the world would go on, young
Ewan dead as his father was dead, or hither and borne,
far from Kinraddie: oh, once she had seen in these
parks, she remembered, the truth, and the only truth
that there was, that only the sky and the seasons endured,
slow in their change, the cry of the rain, the whistle of
the whins on a winter night under the sailing edge of
the moon . . . It was Time himself she had seen,
haunting their tracks with unstaying feet.[62]

As an old man I am very conscious of time's unstaying
feet, knowing how rapidly they are catching up on me. But
I realise now I've been obsessed by time's rush my whole
life long. I would pester my mother to tell me about 'the

olden days', a phrase that haunted me. And the obsession was increased by my love of the movies. I was fascinated by the devices film-makers used to signify the passage of time. They would show the pages of a calendar blowing away in the wind. Or a street scene would dissolve into an older version of the same view, with horses and carts instead of automobiles. But it was the flashback that always got me, as it replayed shots from the movie I had just seen.

I have a clear memory of the flashback from a movie I saw in 1945 when I was eleven. The film was *The Sullivans,* the true story of a large Irish American family of sons, five of whom were killed in the Second World War. I was captivated by the glimpses of the dead brothers at the end of the movie and was stabbed by the sorrow of time's passing. Michael Cimino used the same technique in the sequence at the end of *The Deerhunter,* where the surviving friends sit in a bar and sing 'God Bless America' as the screen flashes images of pre-Vietnam War innocence. The flashback at the end of Francis Ford Coppola's *The Godfather Part II* is even more poignant, recalling Michael's innocence before the inevitable assumption of authority corrupted him. I realise now I've been using this technique when speaking about dead friends at their funerals, such as this address I gave not long ago:

> The movie industry's best artistic invention was the flashback: those sequences at the end of a film when they run clips of the lives of the characters featured in the plot. But the flashback is not an invention of the cinema. It is art imitating life. It is what we all do as

we re-run the movie of the life of one we have loved and lost.

I've been seeing flashbacks of Dougie since the moment a couple of weeks ago when Rena phoned to tell me he had died. And they're all funny, usually terrible jokes he told me, most of them unrepeatable here. It was the way he did it, I remember. I wouldn't have seen him for months, maybe even years, and he'd slope over to me with that gliding, slightly stooped walk he had, a smile playing round his lips. No 'Hi' or 'Hello', just: 'An Angus farmer goes to London on business . . .' I won't repeat that joke, except to say it involved the farmer receiving an unwanted enema at three in the morning in a dodgy hotel near King's Cross.

Here's another clip. I've come to Dundee for an event at the Cathedral where he is now working in his retirement years. At the bun fight in the hall after the service, he approaches me. Again there's no 'Hi' or 'Hello'. I notice he's put on weight. He comes over in that sliding, slightly stooped walk, a smile flickering round his lips, shoves his belly towards me, strokes it sensuously with his right hand and croons, 'solid muscle'. This was the man who told his grandchildren he'd used his braces to bungee-jump from the Eiffel Tower, and that in the olden days he'd fought and won a duel by ramming a stick of rhubarb down his adversary's throat.

So what I remember most about Dougie was his sense of humour. It was Glasgow humour, and it was what bonded us. But it sat alongside a deep religious serious-ness. Dougie was loyal to a traditional kind of Scottish Episcopalianism that has disappeared. The old Scottish Church had nurtured him through tough times in his boyhood, and it had bred in him a passionate conserv-atism with a small 'c'. Conservatives play an important role in the human community. We are a dynamic and restless species, constantly discarding the old and lusting after the new. And much of what we throw away is good and beautiful. Conservatives mourn this prodigal waste of the past and try to hold on to as much of it as they can. Old buildings, old words, old values, old courtesies and old trades are thoughtlessly abandoned by us in our rush through history. Careful conservatives try to hold back the flood of time and rescue what they can from its ruthlessness.

Dougie hated what he saw as the shallow modernising of his beloved Church. Though I was one of the modernisers, our disagreements never came between us. This was partly because I respected the genuine conservative's hatred of the carelessness of many progressives. But it was mainly because we were deter-mined that nothing should ever be allowed to damage the love we had for each other. Dougie also under-stood that the trouble with holding too tightly on to the past is that you preserve the bad as well as the good: ugly prejudices as well as beautiful virtues. Change can bring gain as well as loss. But we should never ignore the cost to those who cherish the memory of what has been lost.

It was typical of Dougie that he weathered the changes and learned to celebrate the best of them. He recognised that it was the role of the thinking conservative to test and challenge change, but once the community had decided upon it to embrace it too. In the end, Dougie would allow nothing to separate him from the Church he had loved since he was a boy. And even though our hearts are breaking, because all we are left with is a film in our heads playing images of his laughter and his love, nothing will separate us from that love either.

Films may have made remembrance of the past and those it has taken from us potently visual, flickering flashbacks, but poets and other writers were doing it long before movies were invented. One of the time-haunted poets I've been reading for years has already appeared several times in these pages, Philip Larkin. He believed that art was essentially the impulse to preserve, the desire to stay those unstaying feet, if only for a moment. In this poem, he is lacerated by time as he looks at an old photograph of a girlfriend:

> Those flowers, that gate,
> These misty parks and motors, lacerate
> Simply by being over; you
> Contract my heart by looking out of date.[63]

But poets are not the only writers waving the train out of the station. Novelists do it as well. And so do playwrights. One of the best of them is Alan Bennett, the champion valedictorian of my generation. And like me he's been doing it all his life. Here's a passage from a recent diary:

That so much of what I've written has been in the valedictory mode ought to make these latter days seem nothing new. I was saying farewell to the world virtually in my teens and my first play (when I was aged 34) was a lament for an England that has gone. My last play (aged 79) was still waving the same handkerchief.[64]

While it is true that artists possess the capacity for recovering and reliving the past to an unusual degree, it is something most of us do. Even if we don't hunt for antiques or collect old books, the chances are that we've held on to a lot of detritus from our own past. I still have my School Certificate from 1950 – only a pass in Greek, I notice – and photographs from my two years' National Service in the Army. Photographs! Larkin was right: nothing lacerates the heart more than poring by lamplight over old photograph albums. And we turn up at reunions, amazed at the changes time has wrought in people we haven't seen for decades – thickened waists and vanished hairlines. Then we attend memorial services to hear dead friends summoned to life for an hour before the church door closes on them forever. We mourn the way time steals everything from us. It takes away our youth. Then those we love. Last of all it comes for us. So it is hardly surprising that it is the main subject of all human art.

It is also religion's great passion. After a life spent wrestling with it, I have learned to understand and use religion also as a human art, the work of an imagination obsessed with time and death. But a big difference between religion and the other arts is that it not only observes and mourns the passing of time, it challenges and defies it in two ways.

It defies the finality of individual death and it refuses the idea that the universe itself may in time die back into emptiness. Let me remember my way back into both of these claims.

***

I found the lines pasted on to the fridge door of a recently widowed friend and have loved them ever since and thought about them often. It was obvious what they meant to her. She longed for the front door to open, and for her husband to come in from the school he taught in, drop his bag on the floor and go to the fridge. What a day! I need a beer. Sometimes she imagined it had happened, and she'd look up eagerly expecting his entrance. Once or twice she thought she'd seen him on the street ahead of her, but as he turned at her call it was a stranger. She knew there was no way back, but she could not stop scenes from the dear, dead past spooling in her mind. No wonder she'd stuck that fragment of verse on to the fridge door.

> If I could turn upon my finger
> The bright ring of time
> The now of then
> I would bring back again.[65]

But for some who mourn a death, it is not a question of bringing back the now of then. For them it has never gone away. That's when the clocks stopped and time stood still. I had a parishioner who kept the easy chair exactly where it was when her husband died in it. He'd been smoking his pipe when he began to feel unwell. So he put it half-smoked into the ash tray on the table beside the chair and died. And twenty years later it was still there, a dried-up plug of old tobacco in it, just as he had left it. That was when the hands on the clock stopped moving for her. She wasn't morbid or weepy about it, but nothing had mattered to her since her husband's death. I doubt if she knew it, but she might have been reciting from one of W.H. Auden's poems:

> He was my North, my South, my East and West,
> My working week and my Sunday rest,
> My noon, my midnight, my talk, my song;
> I thought that love would last forever: I was wrong.
>
> The stars are not wanted now; put out every one;
> Pack up the moon and dismantle the sun;
> Pour away the ocean and sweep up the wood.
> For nothing now can ever come to any good.[66]

If losing the man you've been married to for a lifetime is devastating, the death of a child you've had for only a few years can be worse. Every instinct protests against carrying our own children to the grave. It's a rent in the fabric, a break in the order, a terrible contradiction. No wonder the parent longs to change places with the child in the grave. That's how King David of Israel felt when he heard his rebellious son Absalom had been killed:

> And the king was much moved, and went up to the chamber over the gate, and wept: and as he wept, thus

he said, O my son Absalom, my son, my son Absalom!
Would God I had died for thee, O Absalom, my son,
my son![67]

Religion is at its best and can be at its worst when ministering at the death of children, probably because it is
caught between the longing to comfort and the compulsion
to explain or reconcile such a tragedy. Sometimes the way
it comforts implies an explanation our minds find hard to
accept. As a doubting priest, that's a contradiction I learned
to live with and no longer seek to be rescued from, the
best and the worst of religion. And it is the death of
children that brings it most clearly into focus.

The first funeral of a child I conducted was in February
1960, but I can remember it as if it were yesterday – and
not just because I blundered. I hadn't known the couple
for long when their two-year-old son died. I went with
them to a village outside Lanark to bury him in a tiny
cemetery on the slope of a hill streaked with snow. The
young father insisted on carrying the little white coffin
himself, clutching it fiercely as we trudged to the hole the
gravediggers had dug for his son. I read from the Prayer
Book service for the burial of a child:

Man that is born of a woman hath but a short time to
live, and is full of misery. He cometh up, and is cut
down, like a flower; he fleeth as it were a shadow, and
never continueth in one stay.[68]

Truth but not much comfort there. When it was over, I
put my arm around the mother's shoulders and whispered

a hope the pain would pass. She shoved me away roughly. I want to feel the pain, she cried. How should I not feel the pain for the death of my wee boy? And I want to feel it for ever.

Religion's first instinct in the face of death is to try to console like that – however awkwardly – and it is a particularly strong impulse at the death of a child. Harder than consoling the parents is what to say to a child that knows it is dying. Here the instinct to comfort and reassure is even more overwhelming. It has even been argued that we invented God in order to guarantee or support our longing for life after death. The only consolation we can offer a dying child is that death is not the end – it's the entrance to another life. And since nothing on earth can support or justify that claim, we are forced to put forward the idea of God to guarantee it.

But that's not the right way to put it either. In the moment of encounter with the dying child, theory vanishes, as well as the doubts that must accompany all theory. Facing down this nothingness, the priest is even absent from his own doubts and failures. They are not present because they are irrelevant to the extremity of the situation. The priest is emptied of everything except defiance in the face of absolute loss and becomes, in Auden's phrase, a way of happening, a mouth.[69] And the word the mouth utters is 'NO', even if it is shouted into a void. When I laid my hands gently on the heads of the dying and prayed the presence of a loving God into their minds, in that moment the truth or untruth of my action did not matter. The act contained its own meaning. The act *was* its own meaning. Everything else disappeared except the need to comfort the one afraid to fall into nothing. It was only when the consolation was over that the question of its meaning arose. Looking back, I can see how that dialectic has always been at work in my own experience.

When I was a curate in Glasgow, I became close to the family of an eleven-year-old girl who was dying of leukemia. What do you say to a child who knows she hasn't long to live and is afraid, especially of being taken away from her parents? Apart from being there and offering love and support – hands laid gently on heads in silence – religion also offers God as a future in which the separated will be brought together again. If God is the ultimate reality on whom everything else is dependent or contingent, it follows that in God nothing is ever lost. It is even possible to deal with the difficulty of time for a child's mind. Her parents are young and will live long after she is dead. Will they forget her? But doesn't she see that in God there is no time or change? God is an eternal now. Do you remember times when you were so enthralled by a movie or a book that time stood still for you? It'll be like that. All the pains of separation that time and space impose on us in this life will be resolved in an eternal Here and Now!

Did I believe it? That's the wrong question, though I might not have known it at the time. There was no room for anything else by that bedside, though it was years before I found a way of understanding it. It came to me through one of the greatest books of the twentieth century, *The Last of the Just*, by André Schwarz-Bart, a novel about the Holocaust. At the end of the novel it is 1943, and Ernie Levy with his girlfriend Golda and a band of children he has been protecting are on one of the death trains to Auschwitz. One of the children has just died:

> Ernie said, clearly and emphatically, so that there would be no mistaking him, '*He's asleep* . . . ' Then he picked up the child's corpse and with infinite gentleness laid it on the growing heap of Jewish men, Jewish women, Jewish children, joggled in their last sleep by the jolting of the train.

> 'He was my brother,' a little girl said hesitantly, anxiously, as though she had not decided what attitude it would be best to take in front of Ernie.

> He sat down next to her and set her on his knees. 'He'll wake up too, in a little while, with all the others, when we reach the Kingdom of Israel. There, children can find their parents, and everybody is happy. Because the country we're going to, that's our kingdom you know . . . '

> '*There*,' a child interrupted happily, repeating the words rhythmically as though he had already said, or thought, or heard them several times, '*there, we'll be able to get warm day and night.*'

> 'Yes,' Ernie nodded, 'that is how it will be.'

> '*There*,' said a second voice in the gloom, '*there are no Germans or railway-trucks or anything that hurts.*'

A woman digs her fingernails into Ernie's shoulder . . .

'How can you tell them it's only a dream?' she breathed, with hate in her voice.

Rocking the child mechanically, Ernie gave way to dry sobs. 'Madame,' he said at last, 'there is no room for truth here.'[70]

In a public conversation with Richard Dawkins at the Edinburgh Science Festival some years ago, I quoted those words and asked him what he would have done in the situation. 'The same,' he said. It turns out that there are times when it is impossible to accept the utter finality of death. A child's death is one of them. *There is no room for truth here.* There is only room for the impossible act of consolation.

***

But religion does more than console us in the face of death. It uses its best arts to defy death itself and withstand its power over us. And music is its loudest trumpet. A few years ago, I was at a friend's Solemn Requiem Mass. The setting for the mass was for baritone soloists by the French composer Duruflé. My friend lay in his coffin in the chancel. And my sadness was eased when the young baritone soloist sang Hosanna – save us – again and again over his dead body. I heard it as a protest against the finality of death. Death was a brute power, and it had beaten my friend to the ground. But the beauty of the music defying his death was itself a kind of victory. It reminded me of that young man years ago in Tiananmen Square waving a handkerchief at the huge tank grinding towards him. Death will roll over us all in the end, but it cannot take away our songs. And they strengthen us in ways words never can.

People like me, people of the word brought up in a religion of the word, too easily forget that words can't do everything. We like to believe that everything can be *said*; that there's a verbal equivalent for every human experience. And really great writers almost pull it off. They almost persuade us. Their artistry translates mute emotion into language. Sometimes we shiver with recognition when we read their words because they come so close to expressing what we ourselves have gone through. But they are not art's only form of translation. Some things just can't be said. That's why Edward Hopper, the great American painter of human loneliness, said that if he'd been able to say it he would not have had to paint it. That's even more true of music. And it is why what I am trying to do here is absurd: talking *about* music instead of playing it. All I can do here is to try to bear witness in a few words to what music can express without any words.

As mourners stand in remembrance of their dead at nightfall, what words can convey how a bugle sounding the Last Post from a castle battlement seems to pour the sorrow of all their loss into the wind? Or how an ancient plainchant melody lifting round a church at evensong carries the same ancient sadness and longing?

One of the most remarkable examples of a music that made beauty out of oppression and death is the singing that came from African American slaves in the United States. Think of the longing and pain in the Spirituals and the way they transfigured sorrow into art. One way to connect with their music is through Michael Tippett's oratorio *A Child of our Time*, in which the great spirituals are used like the Passion chorales of Bach to capture and transcend human suffering.

> Steal away, steal away home,
> I ain't got long to stay here . . . [71]

We singers of human sorrow might paraphrase Hopper: if we could say it, we wouldn't have to sing it. But sing it we have, over all the graves of history and against the force that keeps filling them.

And we send out our poetry against death as well. Auden told us that poetry makes nothing happen. True, but it can give defiance a mouth, and that's far from nothing. The mouthiest shout of defiance against death comes from Saint Paul in his First Letter to the Corinthians, the oldest writing in the New Testament, dating from about CE 55, about twenty-five years after the execution of Jesus Christ.

When we first meet Paul, he is a persecutor of those who followed Christ. And it was the word *Christ* that prompted his wrath. *Christos* is the Greek translation of the Hebrew word for Messiah, the agent God would send to establish a new kingdom of justice and peace on earth. It was and remains the fundamental hope of the Jewish people. And not just of the Jews. It is also one of humanity's most persistent dreams – the establishment of a perfect community in which the strife and inequality that characterise our history will be removed at a stroke, and justice and peace will prevail on earth – and death will be no more. The most vivid versions of the dream came from religious visionaries, but there have been secular versions of the messianic hope, and some of them have darkened the politics of my lifetime.

Humans, as reflective animals rarely at peace with themselves, find it hard to live with the muddle and confusion of their nature. So they are always on the lookout for a saviour who will chase all their troubles away. Even the pragmatic and relatively sane political parties of the world's surviving democracies are far from immune to the messianic virus. During periods of accelerating and destructive change, the longing asserts itself again and we start searching the horizon for the one who is to come. It's a theme well rehearsed in the classic Hollywood Western, such as *Shane* in 1953, in which Alan Ladd plays the man from nowhere who rides into a community under threat, destroys the bad guys and rides away again. In 1985, it was reprised more violently by Clint Eastwood in *Pale Rider*. The longing persists. We are always on the lookout for the one who will come and save us from ourselves.

In Paul's time, there were Jews who thought he had come at last and the golden age was about to be inaugurated. They believed that Jesus of Nazareth was the Messiah, the Christ. Hence the name he came to be known by in history, Jesus Christ or Jesus the Messiah. But to their consternation, he did not defeat the powers of this sinful world. He was defeated by them. They executed him on a cross and dumped his body in a criminal's grave. Then his followers described how he appeared to them and told them not to despair. 'Get ready,' he told them, 'I'll be back soon to bring in the longed-for community of righteousness and peace on earth.' To Paul, a devout Jew, the claim was blasphemous, and he was commissioned to hunt down those who made it. But while he was on the chase, he himself had an experience that convinced him Jesus was indeed the Christ, the one who was to come. Here's how he describes it:

> . . . I delivered unto you first of all that which I also received, how that Christ died . . . and that he was buried, and that he rose again the third day . . . and that he was seen of Cephas, then of the twelve: After that, he was seen of above five hundred brethren at once . . . After that he was seen of James; then of all the apostles. And last of all he was seen of me also . . . the least of the apostles, that am not meet to be called an apostle, because I persecuted the church of God.[72]

The thing to note is that his psychic encounter with Christ persuaded Paul that Jesus was the Messiah, but it did not persuade him there was life after death. It did not need to, because that was a conviction he already held. Paul was a Pharisee, a member of a sect in Judaism that believed in the resurrection of the dead, a belief that was by no means universal in Judaism then or now. For Paul, Christ's resurrection was not unique. It was a particular example of a general truth: the dead will rise again. In fact, Paul went on to say that if there was no resurrection of the dead, no life after death, then Jesus Christ couldn't have been raised either:

Now if Christ be preached that he rose from the dead, how say some among you that there is no resurrection of the dead? But if there is no resurrection of the dead, then is Christ not risen . . . and we are found false witnesses of God; because we testified of God that he raised up Christ; whom he raised not up, if so be that the dead rise not.[73]

For Paul, what was unique about the resurrection of Christ was that it signalled the beginning of the end of history and its sorrow. Christ's resurrection was the first move in God's end game. And it would be completed in his lifetime:

Behold, I shew you a mystery; we shall not all sleep, but we shall

all be changed, in a moment, in the twinkling of an eye, at the last

trump: for the trumpet shall sound, and the dead shall be raised

incorruptible, and we shall be changed . . . then shall be brought to

pass the saying that is written, Death is swallowed up in victory. O death, where is thy sting? O grave, where is thy victory?[74]

The important phrases in that passage are 'we shall not all sleep, but we shall all be changed'. Paul is reassuring the followers of Christ that the timetable for God's D-Day is still on, because they were puzzled. They'd been told it would start while all of them were still alive. But it hadn't worked out that way. The trumpet had not sounded, yet some of them had died. Would they miss out on the great day when it came? Paul comforts them. When the trumpet sounds to herald Christ's return, the dead will rise incorruptible from their graves to join in the final victory.

It didn't happen. Still hasn't. Like everyone else, believers in Christ keep on dying. Yet over their graves the Church goes on shouting Paul's defiant questions: 'O death, where is thy sting? O grave, where is thy victory?' And it knows the answers. Hasn't death always been its business? Hasn't it forever watched those graves filling with the dust of its own children? So who can blame it for choosing to confront death not with facts but with poetry?

Death be not proud, though some have called thee
Mighty and dreadful, for, thou art not soe,
For, those, whom thou think'st, thou dost overthrow,
Die not, poore death, nor yet canst thou kill mee.
From rest and sleepe, which but thy pictures bee,
Much pleasure, then from thee, much more must flow,
And soonest our best men with thee doe goe,
Rest of their bones, and soules deliverie.
Thou art slave to Fate, Chance, kings, and desperate men,
And dost with poison, warre, and sicknesse dwell,
And poppie, or charmes can make us sleepe as well,
And better than thy stroake; why swell'st thou then?
One short sleepe past, wee wake eternally,
And death shall be no more; death, thou shalt die.[75]

Religion is at its most compelling when it restrains the urge to explain death away and contents itself with voicing our sorrow and defiance that it keeps beating us into the ground. It feels most authentic when it stops preaching and becomes, instead, our song, our protest, the handkerchief waved against the immense tank looming at the corner of the street. That's when, in Paul's words: 'Death is swallowed up in victory.'

But it is only ever the victory of beauty over *force,* defined by Simone Weil as that '*x* that turns anybody who is subjected to it into a *thing*. Exercised to the limit, it turns man into a thing in the most literal sense: it makes a corpse of him. Somebody was here, and the next minute there is nobody here at all . . .'[76] Death gets us all in the end, but it can never kill our songs. And that is the only victory they give us.

> You strode up the aisle alone,
> unafraid of the hushed gloom,
> stained glass glint from the West
> on your shoulders, and you paused
> in the chancel, slim silhouette
> against the wide East window,
> child in a field of dwindling light,
> listening, it seemed, to the silence.
>
> 'What do you think a church is for?'
> I asked, curious, as we left.
> 'Singing', came your answer,
> quick and sure, 'for singing'.[77]

***

108

Religion not only protests the death of the individual, it also protests the death of the universe, the death of all that flowed from the Big Bang of 14 billion years ago. Science offers various scenarios for how that ultimate death will be. Since it is all unimaginably distant in time – 2.8 billion years away according to one reckoning – it is nothing to get worked up about now. As a physical event, it need not trouble us. The universe as we know it will see us out. But that is not the real issue, or not for me. The issue is what it will have *meant* once it's over. In particular what it will have meant for us, as far as we know the only beings in the universe who can think about these matters. Will it all be lost as if it had never been, 'like tears in rain'?

The phrase comes from Ridley Scott's sci-fi movie *Blade Runner*. Roy is a replicant, played by Rutger Hauer, a humanoid who's been genetically engineered by the Tyrell Corporation to be '*more human than human*', but with a life span of only four years. As Roy feels his powers waning, he looks back on his brief life:

> I've seen things you people wouldn't believe. Attack ships on fire off the shoulder of Orion. I've watched C-beams glitter in the dark near the Tannhauser Gate. All those moments will be lost in time, like tears in rain.

It is hardly surprising that death should pose questions for us not only about the meaning of our own life but about the universe that generated it and in which we spent it. Just as imagining ourselves into the emptiness of death is hard, even harder is it to contemplate the absolute emptiness that will follow the death of the universe, the wiping out of everything, including the minds the universe invented to think about itself. All to be lost like tears in rain!

It is impossible for some of us not to wonder about this paradox. It is why after a lifetime of struggle with, and frequent feelings of revulsion towards, religion I still think of myself as a religious man. But I now practise religion in a way that passionate protagonists on both sides of the God Debate dislike intensely. The frustration I attract reminds me of an incident a few years ago in the debate about gay marriage. Campaigners posted this slogan on the side of London buses:

SOME PEOPLE ARE GAY
GET OVER IT

It was aimed at Christian groups who understood human sexuality not as a spectrum of different shades but as a stark choice between right and wrong, the permitted and the forbidden. Many of us are prone to this kind of binary simplification in moral and theological debate, but it is amplified by those whose favourite discourse is the adversarial. You are either with them or against them. You have to be one thing or the other. There's nothing in between. You certainly can't be both at the same time. This is not only a boring way to look at the world; it is also inaccurate. Nothing is that simple. Louis MacNeice nailed it when he said:

World is crazier and more of it than we think,
Incorrigibly plural.[78]

The tragedy is not just the absurdity of trying to purge the world of its crazy variety, but the pain and hurt it causes those who can't or won't force themselves onto our narrow templates.

The latest collision between the incorrigible plurality of humanity and the dreary compulsion to split everything in two is in our attitude to gender. We now recognise that, like sexuality, gender is fluid and plural. In some people it may never be permanently determined; and it might even shift during a single lifetime. Humans are incorrigibly plural. If we've got a problem with that, it's time we got over it.

It's also time we realised that the human experience of religion is also various and complex. There are those who are firmly in and those who are firmly out of religious institutions. There are those whose belief is strong and those whose unbelief is equally unyielding. And like the majority of the population whose gender and sexuality are clearly printed, they are the ones who claim to define the territory for the rest of us. But there are as many hues on the religious spectrum as there are on gender and sexuality. We should acknowledge that and come to a more generous and comprehensive understanding of this important aspect of human experience.

In the context of the theme of this book – death – there are those for whom religious observance in this life is a way of guaranteeing their status in the next. Their gaze is on the world beyond and how to get there. But for some of us life after death has little attraction, and we even doubt it exists. It is life before death we concentrate our attention on. We want to make it more just and abundant and joyful for everyone. And some of us find that medi-tating on religion's best narratives, and listening to its wisest teachers, and being moved by its music and poetry, strengthens us for that work. We don't want to prise others out of their systems of belief or unbelief any more than we want to be boxed into them. Even if we disagree on the best deal after death, why can't we agree on a good deal for everyone before death? Anyway, the gulf between us is not as wide as it may appear. Religions that believe we go on to life after death all say its quality will depend on how we lived before death. Do good in this world and good will be done unto thee in the next, is the mantra. So whatever the final calculation, this world becomes a better place – exactly what those of us with little interest in eternal life want as well. Everyone wins.

But in my experience, if you adopt this dialectical approach to religion, you get caught in the crossfire of its main protagonists. Both the champions and the despisers of religion attack you with equal contempt. It's the binary game again. You have to be one thing or the other. You can't be both at the same time or anything in between. Well, tough. Some of us are. Get used to it.

However, there is more to my attitude to the wars of religion than the desire for a ceasefire to help the wounded. The big question at the centre of the conflict troubles me as well, though I cannot resolve it, cannot situate myself permanently at either pole of the discussion. The binary nature of the choice feels false to my experience. Is this a particularly Scottish tension? Hugh MacDiarmid certainly thought it marked the Scottish character. In his book on *Scottish Eccentrics*, published in 1936, he talked about 'the

Caledonian Antisyzygy' – an antisyzygy being the presence of opposing or competing polarities within the same entity. And it has become a cliché in describing our cultural history: Stevenson's Jekyll and Hyde being the proverbial example. Wherever the affliction comes from, its main symptom is intense discomfort with any claim to absolute finality in answering the big question the universe poses for us.

The theologian Paul Tillich said that being religious meant asking the ultimate question of the meaning of the universe, even if we arrived at an answer that hurt us. An answer that hurts me is that ultimately it means nothing because there never was anyone there to mean it. It just happened. The riddle is that, without having any meaning itself, the universe generated human creatures with a need for meaning, who then projected meaning onto its speech-less blankness. They thought it had spoken to them, had disclosed itself. But it was their own words they were hearing, their own longing they were fulfilling. It was all in the mind, the human mind, the only mind the universe possesses. That is an answer that hurts me. Because I think it may be right. It was an answer that also hurt the Spanish philosopher Miguel de Unamuno. In wrestling with the impossible idea of his own non-existence, his own anni-hilation by death and the annihilation of the whole universe, he wrote an extraordinary book that is not so much a philosophy or theology of death as a great cry of protest against it, a great NADA! He was one of death's deniers honest enough to admit he needed God in order to guarantee his own immortality. In his book *The Tragic Sense of Life,* he quotes from the Italian philosopher Leopardi:

A time will come when this Universe and Nature itself will be extinguished. And just as of the grandest kingdoms and empires of mankind and the marvellous things achieved therein, very famous in their own time, no vestige or memory remains today, so, in like manner, of the entire world and of the vicissitudes and calamities of all created things there will remain not a single trace, but a naked silence and a most profound stillness will fill the immensity of space. And so before ever it has been uttered or understood, this admirable and fearful secret of universal existence will be obliterated and lost.[79]

That was the possibility that haunted me as I prepared to speak at the funeral of my friend Malcolm. Malcolm had wanted us all to remember him laughing. It was certainly an impossible laugh to forget, a great explosion of merriment and the huge heart it expressed. Even more important to me than his laugh was his smile when you met him. It was a smile of absolute welcome. This was a man who cherished his friends and kept them close, and his smile was the sign that his heart welcomed you in again with delight. That smile was there for his friends to the end as he lay on the sad height of his death bed.

There was laughter in his dying as in his living; but his had been a hard dying, bravely endured; and it would have been dishonest to ignore it or try to conceal it. This is what I found myself saying:

Malcolm was a fiercely honest man, a man who refused to hide from following truth as he saw it; so we should not hide from this truth either: his was a hard dying. We all owe the universe a death, but not everyone owes it a hard one, and Malcolm certainly didn't. His wife Marion captured its pain in her poem about his last months:

Fresh from a family luncheon,
Short-cutting through the cemetery,
He found himself stranded in red-hot pain,
Unable to move:
The first step on a slow journey to a dead end.

Losses piled up unannounced, huge and mean.
Promises of better times flickered and fled.
Each treatment stole vigour from limbs and life.
The triple bypass now beat mercilessly.
And hope seeped from our hearts.

We learned to live with the downward path,
To be grateful for freedom by buggy.
For the jab that distanced the pain, even while
    holding onto the agony.
We learned to be thankful for being shielded for
    so long from the knowledge that it could be like
    this at the end.
And sometimes our hearts shone as they bled,
    and we were thankful for that too.

So Malcolm's dying forces a question from us: how are we to find meaning in the agony of such a good and life-enhancing man? Christian Faith has its confident answer, and those of us within the Christian tradition are familiar with its claims and their power to console, even if, like Malcolm, we have come to doubt them and the confidence with which they are proclaimed.

But if we hold to the old consolations and believe that all shall be well in the end, all wrongs ultimately righted and tears wiped from every eye, there is still a difficulty in explaining how, in the meantime, the creator has ended up making us traverse a universe so steeped in pain and loss and so packed with grief. We may believe things will come right in the long run, but what is there to say about the short run? In particular, what is there to say about the meaning of this man's life and his hard dying? I can think of three things to say at a time like this.

First, even if the universe is ultimately without meaning, and even if we dismiss religion's consolation, in the words of the poet Philip Larkin as:

> That vast moth-eaten musical brocade.
> Created to pretend we never die . . . [80]

we are left with the paradox that amidst the tumults and plagues and cruelties of existence, the universe has also given birth to love and laughter – both of them strongly embodied in the life of the man we mourn and celebrate today. I don't want to push the claim too far, but is there not something unexpectedly gracious about a universe that can prompt a strong, confident, creative man like Malcolm to turn from the making of board games, at which he was a celebrated artist, and turn himself into an internationally respected cartographer of the strange land of dementia and a sympathetic guide through the dark valley of ageing?

My second point follows from that. Even if the universe ultimately means nothing and comes to nothing; even if we agree with the philosopher Leopardi that a time will come when this Universe and Nature itself will be extinguished . . . and this admirable and fearful secret of universal existence will be obliterated and lost; even if that is to be the final truth of existence itself; I believe we can say that a life like Malcolm's was its own meaning and justification, if only as an act of defiance of the void that awaits us all. Even if all comes to nothing, this man's life, this confident, creative, compassionate life has brought meaning out of the abyss, and in celebrating it today we will not let it go to waste.

It is right to mourn Malcolm's death and to cry at losing one we loved so much. But we should also let his joyful living and brave dying strengthen us in our own struggle to live well; and when our own time comes to die as bravely as he did.

Go from us, good friend: you have strengthened us for the struggle, and your laughter we will never forget.

As I left the pulpit, the thought of the void giving birth to a life as generous as Malcolm's – and then deleting it

– continued to trouble me. Even if Leopardi is right and the experiment of being was empty of meaning from the beginning, and even if the universe is destined to be sucked back into the nothingness it came from and be succeeded by a naked silence and a profound stillness; then we will have proved ourselves better than the void that spawned us, because of what we ourselves created: great music, torrents of it, poured out down the centuries; great words, rivers of them, all trying to express the mystery of our own existence; paintings that captured its loneliness and grandeur; and acts of loving kindness that defied the sneer of the abyss that swallowed them. And isn't it strange that such beauty and purpose came from such emptiness?

So why be shocked when some of us find ourselves answering the question of ultimate meaning with a NO and a YES in the same breath and at the same time? That's the antisyzygy in which some of us find ourselves. And yes, it hurts. It's the pain that comes with being human. That's why Unamuno advised us that, even if it is nothingness that awaits us and the universe, we humans should so live that it will be an unjust fate.

VI

THE DAY AFTER

The American philosopher Arthur Danto described the human animal in a Latin phrase as an *ens representans*, a being that represents the world back to itself, a being that mirrors being. And we can't help doing it. Give children crayons and a sheet of paper, and they'll draw mummy and daddy and the cat on the mat before the fireplace. Listen to people on the bus going home from work, and they'll be telling their day over again to their friends. All human art flows from this compulsion to represent or describe or make over again all the worlds we experience. And the best artists do it to a miraculous degree. We say of them what Samuel Beckett said of the writings of James Joyce: they were not *about* the thing; they were the thing itself.[81] Great art does not tell or talk about its subject. It *shows* it, makes it present. It is all part of the human passion to preserve at least the memory of the past before it hurtles into oblivion. Writers do it. Photographers do it. And so do painters. This is how John Berger described their purpose:

> The portraitist contests the mortality of his sitter. The landscape painter contests the ceaseless movement of nature; the history painter the forgetting of history; and

the still life painter the dispersal of objects. His antag-
onists are decay, the bailiff and the junk merchant.[82]

Religion does it too. At his last supper with his disciples the
night before he died, Jesus blessed bread and wine and gave
it to his companions at table in these words from their
Greek translation in the gospels: *'touto poiete eis tēn emen
anamnesin'*, 'do this in remembrance of me'.[83] In that quota-
tion, the Greek word *anamnesin* is worth thinking about. It's
translated as *remembrance,* a word that has lost some of the
power of the original. To us, remembering suggests the
backward look. We sit under the lamp with the photograph
album and see ourselves as we were and others who are no
longer with us. But sometimes the experience does not feel
like a backwards glance, a look over the shoulder. Through
the chemistry of longing, someone from the past comes
alive to us again. We imagine them in the street ahead of
us and have to halt ourselves from crying out. We catch
ourselves saying wait till I tell her *this*, forgetting for a
moment that she's gone forever. That's why people take
part in séances with psychics who claim to be able to make
contact with the dead. Raising the dead is an ancient art,
and even the Bible, which disapproves of the practice,
contains accounts of it. In one of them, King Saul, perplexed
about the challenges that face him as leader of Israel, tries
to summon up his old adviser Samuel to help him:

> Then Saul said to his servants, 'Seek out for me a woman
> who is a medium, that I may go to her and enquire of
> her.' And his servants said to him, 'Behold, there is a
> medium at Endor.'

So Saul disguised himself and put on other garments, and went, he and two men with him; and they came to the woman by night. And he said, 'Divine for me by a spirit, and bring up for me whomever I shall name to you.' The woman said to him, 'Surely you know what Saul has done, how he has cut off the mediums and the wizards from the land. Why then are you laying a snare for my life to bring about my death?' But Saul swore to her by the Lord, 'As the Lord lives, no punishment shall come upon you for this thing.' Then the woman said, 'Whom shall I bring up for you?' He said, 'Bring up Samuel for me.' When the woman saw Samuel, she cried out with a loud voice; and the woman said to Saul, 'Why have you deceived me? You are Saul.' The king said to her, 'Have no fear; what do you see?' And the woman said to Saul, 'I see a god coming up out of the earth.' He said to her, 'What is his appearance?' And she said, 'An old man is coming up; and he is wrapped in a robe.' And Saul knew that it was Samuel, and he bowed with his face to the ground, and did obeisance.[84]

Though attempts to summon or use the dead in this way have been banned by many religions, they have rarely been consistent in their disapproval. We have already seen that in Catholic doctrine the prayers of the living were believed to assist the dead on their way through purgatory. The reverse was also true. It was thought that the prayers of the dead could assist those still alive on earth. Because it was believed that those holy souls who had entered heaven at death were now in a position to petition God on behalf of the living, much the way a favoured courtier might persuade a monarch to promote a friend. Intercessory prayer of this sort became specialised, and it was believed that individual saints had particular skills when it came to aiding human need. Going on a journey? Get the protection of the saint who looked after travellers. Lost a precious possession? Go to the saint for lost property. Cannot beget a child? There was a saint whose intercession could help with that. It wasn't exactly what is now called spiritualism – the belief that the living can be in direct contact with the dead – but it wasn't that far from it either.

In the middle of the nineteenth century, the Spiritualist movement in the United States formed itself into an organised denomination. Spiritualists believed that the souls of the dead were located on an etheric plane parallel to the physical universe, which was accessible to psychics like the one Saul consulted at Endor. A spiritualist service was a séance enfolded within a liturgy. There would be prayers and readings as in a conventional act of worship, but the real focus was on communication with the dead.

Around the same time in Victorian England, some prominent members of society became interested in spiritualism for scientific reasons. They formed the Society for Psychical Research to examine paranormal phenomena to see if it could prove the existence of life beyond the grave. The method they adopted to gather proof of life on the other side was a system of automatic or spirit writing called cross-correspondence. The idea was that when members of the Society for Psychical Research died, they would use spirit writing to get back in touch with those still alive, and in this way they could cross-check any claims made. The philosopher John Gray said all their carefully designed experiments achieved was a reflection of their own subconscious longings. It turned out that the after-world was very like the one these Victorian researchers had left behind. And dying was like moving from one wing of a great English country-house to another.[85]

The slaughter of the Great War gave added impetus to the Spiritualist movement in both its ecclesiastical and scientific modes. Most cities in the West will have at least one Spiritualist church. There are still some universities with departments that do research into the paranormal. And famous mediums still pack out theatres with their public séances and demonstrations of psychic power. Whatever we make of all this, it shows that in human experience the dead fascinate the living. One way or another they continue to intrude into our lives.

***

And sometimes they appear unprompted. When I began pondering this, I went first to my Greek New Testament. I wanted to reflect on the meaning of *anamnesis* in Christian thinking about the dead in that passage about the Last Supper. Then I decided to check the Latin as well, so I went to my Latin New Testament. And a gate to the past opened before me. The Latin New Testament I consulted asserted its own past as well as incidents in my own. I remembered buying it in Lent 1969 from Thin's bookshop on South Bridge in Edinburgh, just opposite the Old Quad of the University. Thin's – as the bookshop then was – had a rambling second-hand book department in its deep, cluttered basement. That's where I picked it up. It was a handsome, slightly scuffed, leather-bound volume with gilt-edged pages, small enough to slip into a pocket – *vigesimo-quarto,* in printers' lingo. It had been published in 1911. And it had been a gift. On the inside cover, there was the autograph of Alexander Stewart, St Mary's College, St Andrews – and then pasted on the flyleaf at the front was a card that read:

WITH THE
REV. H.J. WHITE'S
KIND REGARDS

And in Alexander Stewart's handwriting on the bottom right-hand corner of the card was the date, Jan. 1912. It summoned the past from before the Great War. Who was Alexander Stewart, a common enough name in Scotland? Who was the Rev. H.J. White, whose address, as the bottom left-hand corner of his visiting card informed me, was 33 Lexham Gardens, W? Did that unattached W suggest a London address? The mystery is solved on the title page. It tells me in Latin that Henricus Iulianus White was one of the editors of this version of Saint Jerome's fourth-century translation of the Bible into Latin. It also tells me that he was Professor of the Interpretation of the New Testament at King's College, London – so my guess was right, a London address. My next guess is that the Rev. H.J. White had sent a copy of his new work of scholarship to Alexander Stewart of St Andrew's University, tucking his business card inside as a 'with compliments of the author' slip. Alexander Stewart then glued it on to the flysheet with the date he received it. My third guess is that Stewart too was a theologian, and a quick bit of research proves it. And not just another theologian; he was a very distinguished one. At the time of the gift, he was Principal and Professor of Divinity at the University of St Andrews and a former Moderator of the General Assembly of the Church of Scotland. He didn't live long after receiving Professor White's gift in 1912. He died unexpectedly in the summer of 1915. H.J. White lived on till 1934.

A dead world has been conjured to life on my desk by a hundred-year-old book I picked up for thirty-five pence nearly fifty years ago. How did it end up in Thin's? I reckon that after his death in 1915, Professor Stewart's library was passed on to his children. A couple of generations later, whatever was left was sold to a book dealer and some of it ended up in Thin's labyrinthine basement. As I hold this remnant of Alexander Stewart's library from 1912 and turn its pages to find the verses I am looking for, a card falls out. And another memory floods in. It was the requiem card for a beloved friend whose funeral I had conducted twenty-five years before.

My memory of her had gone, yet there she was again, vividly present in my mind. Breast cancer had killed her. And it took its time. It had reduced her beauty to ashes except for the bright shining of her eyes. Her metaphor for death had been the train not the bus. She knew she'd have to board alone, but she wanted me there up to the last moment. 'Make sure you buy a platform ticket,' she warned me. Though platform tickets were no longer issued, I knew what she meant. Compartments in the old trains opened directly onto the platform, so tickets had to be checked before passengers boarded. And if you wanted to see someone onto the train, you needed a ticket to get through the barrier to the platform. It meant you could stay beside a friend till she opened the compartment door and went aboard. That's where she wanted me, as close as I could get to her departure. I was there when the train drew in and she boarded. So how could I have forgotten her? I feel faithless and helpless. Time not only steals those we love; it even steals our memories of them. Their graves fill with the dust of the years, and we forget them. Then one day we come upon a card in an old book and a long dead friend steps through the door of memory into the present. And we mourn again.

It is the absoluteness of the loss we feel after a death that stuns us.

At last I am alone . . . Now there is nothing left. All your papers have been taken away. Your clothes have gone. Your room is bare. In a few months no traces will be left . . . and never again, however long I lookout of the window, will I see your tall thin figure walking across the park past the dwarf pine, past the stumps, and then climb the ha-ha and come across the lawn. Our jokes have gone forever.[86]

It is Carrington's *forever* in that extract from her diaries about the death of Lytton Strachey that hits us. How can we bear such absolute losses, such complete disappearances? What we have done in our grief is to craft arts of mourning and remembrance to hold open the door before it closes forever on the beloved dead. Religion has its own memorial arts, and the phrase from Luke's

Gospel I was searching for when I found my friend's requiem card captures both their strength and elusiveness: *touto poiete eis tēn emen anamnesin* . . . do this in remembrance of me.[87]

Anamnesis is a profound word, deeper than the simple act of remembrance. For Plato, anamnesis lay at the heart of his theory of learning. Like the sages of India, he believed that our souls had been repeatedly incarnated, and, since we had all forgotten what we had known in previous lives, learning was a process of recall or rediscovery of what had been lost. You do not have to believe in reincarnation to go on finding truth in that idea. We let too much of what is good and beautiful sink into the unremembered past, even the lives of those we loved. And what we are doing when we use our imagination to remember the dead is to bring them to life again, if only for a moment. Not in a séance that magically summons them to appear in our midst, however unwillingly. But through an art of remembrance or anamnesis that is so lovingly felt we say of it that it isn't *about* the person; it is the person herself.

In Christianity, this idea of making someone present again after death was mainly applied to Jesus Christ in the Eucharist, the service that commemorated his last supper when he told them to break bread and drink wine as his anamnesis. The Eucharist was not *about* Jesus; it was Jesus himself present in the forms of bread and wine. Jesus Christ also became the dominant presence in Christian funerals. The Church was more intent on proclaiming the future that awaited the departed in heaven than on remembering the life they had lived on earth. The readings and prayers were all about the life to come not the life that had just ended:

> Almighty God, with whom do live the spirits of them that depart hence in the Lord, and with whom the souls of the faithful, after they are delivered from the burden of the flesh, are in joy and felicity: We beseech thee that it may please thee, of thy gracious goodness, shortly to accomplish the number of thine elect, and to hasten thy kingdom; that we, with all those that are departed in the true faith of thy holy Name, may have our perfect consummation and bliss, both in body and soul, in thy eternal and everlasting glory . . . [88]

Prayers of consolation were also offered for those who mourned, but the emphasis was on the prospects for the departed. Funerals did not look back; they looked forward. And the prospect could be forbidding.

The most striking of Christian funeral services was the Catholic Church's traditional Requiem Mass for the Faithful Departed. It was a special version of the normal Eucharist with subtle shifts of emphasis and tone. It was celebrated in the presence of the corpse, for whom it was a cry to God for mercy. And it was more sombre than the normal mass. The colour of the vestments was black, sometimes edged with gold to suggest the hope of resurrection; and instead of creamy beeswax, the candles were unbleached and dark orange in colour. But the most tremendous addition was the great choral sequence, *Dies Irae* or Day of Wrath, a dramatic meditation on judgement. As we have already noticed, this fear of eternal damnation hung like a funeral pall over medieval and late medieval Christian thought. The *Dies Irae* was a plea of the frightened soul to the merciful heart of Christ:

> Day of wrath and doom impending,
> David's word with Sybil's blending!
> Heaven and earth in ashes rending.
>
> O, what fear man's bosom rendeth,
> When from heaven the Judge descendeth,
> On whose sentence all dependeth.
>
> Death is struck, and nature quaking,
> All creation is awaking,
> To its judge an answer making.
>
> Lo! The book exactly worded,
> Wherein all hath been recorded;
> Thence shall judgement be awarded.
>
> What shall I, frail man, be pleading?
> Who for me be interceding,
> When the Just are mercy needing?[89]

It is not often heard in churches nowadays, but even in the concert hall when the great classical requiems are performed, it can send a shiver down our spines. Even if we do not believe in the doom the great hymn fears, there is something about death itself that summons us to consider the heedlessness of our own lives. It prompts us to self-reflection before it is too late.

Even in religious funerals today the emphasis has shifted from the future that awaits the dead to the life they actually lived while on earth. That is certainly the style in memorial services for famous people, where they summon the dead to make their last appearance on the stage before disappearing into the wings forever. In humanist services – increasingly prevalent today – there is no focus on the future life because it is neither desired nor expected. The emphasis is all on re-presenting the life that has ended in a final anamnesis. And sometimes the dead are given the last word. In a non-religious funeral I conducted recently, the deceased had carefully crafted a message for me to read in her name. It was a song of gratitude for having lived and a message of love to her partner and daughter, both of whom were immensely comforted by it. Unlike the funerals I conducted as a young priest, where the form was strictly set by the Prayer Book, the ones I lead today are usually specially crafted to reflect the life that has ended.

This can be hard if the life being remembered was incomplete or unfulfilled. That said, it is probably the unfulfilled life that speaks best to those of us who feel we didn't make the most of ours either – and now it is too late. Thinking about lives that didn't quite happen helps us remember that, although we didn't deal the hand, we had to play the cards life gave us. The death of a friend who had been Director of Music at Old Saint Paul's in Edinburgh when I was Rector there in the 1970s gave me a chance to reflect on the grace of the apparently unfulfilled life:

The novelist Rebecca West claimed that artistic genius was 'the abnormal justifying itself . . . those who know that they are for whatever reason condemned by the laws of life . . . make themselves one with life by some magnificent act of creation'. West was saying that creativity had one of its roots in a disconnection between prevailing conventions and the reality of the artist's life. That dissonance was the grit in the soul that became the pearl of great price: wonderful art.[90]

I don't want to romanticise Alistair, but I have a strong feeling that all the turbulent and conflicting elements in his character were reconciled when he sat himself down at an organ console and emptied himself into the music. Not being a musician, I can only guess at what that must have felt like. But I too have had moments in my life when I was emptied into something larger, something that cancelled or absorbed the clamours of my own nature and gave me a rest from myself. The technical name for this is ecstasy, which means to get out of or off your own ego with all its needs and posturing and dissonances.

I can remember many occasions in this church when we'd got to the end of a great hymn, and Alistair would zoom or lift off into a piece of breath-taking improvisation. And you sensed that the awkward, abrasive yet intensely kind man on the organ stool was far away from himself and had become music and resolution and beauty. He had been 'justified', to use a word with a strong redemptive echo in Christianity, a word that promises that our struggles and self-loathing are destined to be caught up into an enormous mercy and grace that says yes to us just as we are and accepts us even though we feel ourselves to be unacceptable. I don't know if musical theorists would agree with me on this, but it seems to me that Fauré's Requiem captures and expresses that same experience of human reconciliation, which is why it is the right setting for Alistair's farewell. It reconciles us to all the dying and going forth that is the human lot, and brings forth beauty from loss: it justifies us, brings meaning out of brokenness and carries us home.

Maybe his genius for improvisation is the clue to understanding Alistair and his conflicts with authority over the years. Improvisation is the art of departing from fixed rules and making up new music now heard for the first time; and this is something the authoritarian personality hates. Authoritarians like rules and regulations; they like things done the way they have always been done; that's why when they get control of institutions they resist change. Their motto is: do nothing for the first time. It is improvisers like Alistair who bring necessary change to moribund societies. Blessed are the improvisers for they make all things new.

***

So those we love leave us. We see them no longer, but we try to hold on to them as long as we can. In their funerals and memorials, we do our best to contain and express the meaning of the lives we have lost forever. Before the service, we sit in our chairs thinking about them, trying to compress their essence into a few hundred words before closing the curtains on yet another life. Like Dora Carrington, we remember their jokes, the way they walked, their shape. We don't hide from their flaws. In fact, we discover that they were part of why we loved them. They touched the incomplete places in our own souls. Suddenly we realise that what annoyed us about them is what we'll miss most of all — their quirks and absurdities. And we wonder all over again if we told them how much we loved them.

It is a great pity we don't know
When the dead are going to die
So that, over a last companionable
Drink, we could tell them
How much we liked them.

Happy the man who, dying, can
Place his hand on his heart and say:
'At least I didn't neglect to tell
The thrush how beautifully she sings.'[91]

Then it's the day after the funeral. Our friends have gone back to their lives. We want to go back to ours but no longer know where it is. Its meaning has gone. We are no longer living as we did before. We are grieving. We have known grief before, of course. There have been other losses. But none like this. No other loss prepared us for the loss of death because there is no loss like it. *Our jokes have gone forever!* Death is an absolute loss. Because she realised she could not live without Lytton Strachey, Carrington killed herself – clumsily, with a shotgun. Grief can kill. Quickly, as in Carrington's case, or in the slow emotional death of enduring sorrow that takes the life out of life.

What *is* grief, this *x* that hits us like an express train? Answering that question in writing is like trying to put the experience of music into words. It doesn't easily translate into the language of definition, though we can glimpse it in the experiences of others. We heard it in David's lament for his son Absalom: *Would God I had died for thee*. We saw it when Carrington pressed the shotgun against her stomach and reached for the trigger to silence grief forever. Grief has as many layers and textures as there are individual circumstances, but its essence is a stunned and sorrowing bewilderment that 'somebody was here and the next minute there is nobody here at all'. It is not only the experience of loss; it is bafflement at the loss and a sense of its impossibility. *This cannot be happening.*

We may not be able to define or describe grief in words, but we can hear it. It has a voice, a sound of its own making, its own music. We describe the words that express this sound, this music, as onomatopoeic. The meaning is in the sound. Hear it, and you know immediately what it is. *Keening* is one of the words. *Ululating* is another. They are the sounds of loss, its ideomotor effect, and even the most stoical find it hard to repress them, battling tears and suppressing sobs, denying grief expression and escape, bottling it in. Sooner or later it will have to be released, do its work of protest, make its music heard, or it will divert its pain into self-harm and torment. And that's when grief counsellors have to do their work, unclogging the memory, helping to release the long-silenced scream.

Any death prompts its own measure of grief and pain. But how the life was lost can add complexity to the grief and extend it, sometimes beyond resolution. Death by suicide, especially a violent and dramatic one, will pile extra layers of anger and guilt onto grief's already heavy load. Why didn't they share their despair? Why didn't we read the signals? Why couldn't we keep them happy? Why weren't we enough for them? How could they do this to us?

A death caused by medical negligence can add a sense of betrayal to grief's chemistry. We trusted them with this precious life. We gave it into their care. And the enquiries that follow may prolong its pain for years.

The death of a child can exile its parents in the far country of despair. Sometimes it splits them apart. They accuse themselves of failing to protect their child and give their own life for it: *Would God I had died for thee.* I still see that tiny white coffin on a snowy day in Lanark a lifetime ago. And I remember the funeral of a stillborn child in Edinburgh whose mother kept saying it was not her daughter's death she mourned but her future, a future she memorialised in her own life. *She would be eighteen today.*

And prejudice can add its poison to the mix. I recall the angry grief of a parishioner whose partner's body was taken away by his parents and buried privately without any acknowledgement that he was gay.

There was the woman who told me how she had slipped into the back of the cathedral during the Solemn Requiem

Mass for the famous man who had been her lover, and how she had left before anyone could notice her and wonder who she was. Now she was alone with a grief that dare not speak its name.

Grief is shattering, but it can be survived if we let ourselves experience it. It has to be *done*, not bypassed, muffled or diverted. An important part of doing it is anamnesis, the work of remembrance, of going back over the life we have lost as if searching for clues that might solve the mystery of its departure. We can usually do this best with our relatives and friends. But we may have to go to a counsellor or a priest if we get stuck, or if there are issues we can only explore with someone who will hold them in confidence.

The dying can help our grieving. They will help if they think ahead and prepare the way for their absence in our lives. The only future life any of us can be certain of is the one we'll have in the memory of those we shall leave behind. Why not plan it before we go? Such as leaving letters that tell them how much we loved them and how much they meant to us. Or by leaving instructions about the funeral we want – as long as we realise that it is as much for them as it is about us. Don't mess with their grief by being too prescriptive, like the man I knew who insisted that no eulogy should be delivered at his funeral, thereby frustrating those of us who wanted to celebrate his distinguished life. He left detailed directions about the music and readings he wanted, but forbade any words about himself. It felt like everyone was there except him. He couldn't be bothered to turn up at his own funeral. Plan ahead, and you will help good grief do its work of sorrow and remembering. And keep your plans up to date.

I've had to change my funeral plans several times because I keep outliving the friends I wanted to participate in it.

The dying can also hinder our grieving. They can make grief harder for the bereaved than it might otherwise be. They can poison someone's future by forcing them to fret over an unhealed past. Sometimes this is the legacy the dead actually want to bequeath the living. They want their anger to pulse down the years after they are gone. I think of the man who learned on the day his father's will was read how much he had been despised; and how carefully his father had propelled that hatred into the future. He was excluded from the will in an act calculated to deliver a wound he would feel for the rest of his days. How can an act like that ever be reconciled? What must it feel like to know your father wanted you to carry his hatred in your head till your own death?

Jesus told us not to let the sun go down on our wrath, to mend a hurt before putting out the light. All the more reason to heal injuries before the light goes out forever. Don't let death go down on your wrath because you meant to get round to healing that old hurt – but never did. Now it may never heal. Religious visions of the abode of the dead as places of eternal bliss or eternal woe can be given a helpful secular meaning. The dead can be thought of as living on in the lives of those who remember them either in peace or in torment, depending on how their relations were at the end. The dead may be gone but their karma goes marching on. Try to make good karma for those you leave behind. Don't leave in a way that will corrupt your own memory.

Whatever the circumstances that attend a death, grief

has to be *done*, it has to be expressed. The pain has to be endured. We have to get used to the fact that someone who was there has now gone forever. We can leave his pipe in the ash tray if we like. We can't avoid the fact that his chair is empty and his jokes have gone forever. Friends can help if they listen to us and let our grief be voiced, however angry it sounds. It is often in grief that the bereaved discover who their real friends are. Some people can't cope with the grief of others because they can't face death and don't want to think about it. There are many stories about new widows and widowers seeing friends coming towards them in the street who suddenly dash to the other side rather than meet them. As if fearing the contagion of death, they avoid all contact with the bereaved.

Gradually, almost without knowing it, our energy shifts from the past to the present; from the way things were to the way they are. The will to live that is in the heart of every creature asserts itself again. And life overcomes death, even a death we thought we would never recover from. We may even fall in love again. We may pour our hearts into another life as completely as into the one whose death we thought we could not survive. The future opens before us, and we turn towards it. We start living again. If you live as long as I have, you see this happening again and again. You see sorrow unfolding into joy as the years bring their changes. One of the privileges of the priest's life is to be present at both ends of these transformations. Not long ago a young man came to see me with his fiancée. More than thirty years before I had conducted his mother's funeral. Would I marry them? This is what I said at their wedding on a hill in Fife:

Forgive me if I begin on a personal note. In 1975, when I was Rector of Old St Paul's on the Royal Mile in Edinburgh, a young nurse called Connie Cuthbertson came in to see me. It was the death of her brother Bobby that brought her in my direction. She told me of her grief and the grief of her parents, who had now lost two sons, Andrew having died in 1958. But life moved on and her sorrow turned to joy when she and Norman married in Old St Paul's one snowy day in February, and they went over the Forth to run a farm and grow a family on this hill.

I was away from Edinburgh for six years and came back in 1986 to discover that Connie was dying. I came to see her here and something she said captured the essence of her personality. Her hair had fallen out, but she told me with a smile that she spread it on the bushes in the garden so that the birds could use it for their nests. That incident captured the grace, kindness and humour of her soul. Death took her and again there was sorrow in her family. But sorrow was again followed by joy when Norman married a young widow called Trish and she brought her sons into this family of large men, the Niven boys all built on the scale of Connie's gentle giant of a father, Robin Cuthbertson. Today that story of loss and the love that overcame it passes another milestone, as Graham and Amy bind their lives together whatever the future may hold for them.

The most moving thing about a wedding is the way it gathers scattered elements of the past and brings them together into a new future. Amy's story also has its losses and its intriguing connections. Her loving and selfless father Andrew died nearly three years ago after a history of heart disease. Drew, as he was known in the family, was a metallurgist, who in his twenties had worked for a time for Trish's father. Just file that wee coincidence away for a second, because there are more to come. It's as if some benign force in nature was gently nudging these two fine young people together. And fine they are, each of them working selflessly to care for our planet and all the living creatures whose home it is. They didn't know it, but slowly they were being drawn together. They had friends and interests in common. They liked the same bands – one of them, Whisky Kiss, playing here today. They went to the same concerts, socialised in the same pubs. They even lived at different ends of the same street. Then one night with a group of friends in a pub in Tollcross their paths finally crossed, a spark was lit and the courtship began. And being the brave, adventurous people they are, when it came, the marriage proposal wasn't made on Blackford Hill or in a bar in Bruntsfield. It happened on a finger of the Southern Patagonian Ice Field in the distant reaches of South America, as far from Leamington Terrace as you can get.

So these two beautiful and idealistic young lives were joined. And we have come here today to witness and celebrate their love and offer them the encouragement of our support as they begin their lives together. As well as being an act of promised love, a wedding service is an act of courage in which two people pledge their lives together for the future no matter what it holds. We know that human life can never fully escape sorrow and may even encounter terrible loss. But we also know that the love people have for each other can withstand whatever the future brings and guide them through its storms.

We will surround Amy and Graham with our love as they set out on their journey together today. But before we send them on into the future, we want to look back at two great souls they love but see no longer, Graham's mother Connie and Amy's father Drew. Though in one sense they are no longer with us, in another sense they are: because they are present in their children, as they will be in their children's children. So we look back for a moment now, but not in sorrow. Only in joy for what they gave and what their children will carry of them into the long years ahead. And to celebrate that undying link with the past I now invite Amy and Graham to light these two candles for Connie and Drew, absent today but carried always in our hearts.

VII

THE LAST BUS

I was phoned recently by someone who had been commissioned by a newspaper to write my obituary. There was a fact he wanted to check and couldn't find the answer to. Would I mind helping him? I was happy to. And it got me thinking about the important role obituaries can play in helping us prepare for death.

We don't any of us know the date of our own death. And it is silly to think it has already been fixed by the Omniscient Registrar in the sky. But there is a date out there of which in the future they will say, that's the day you died. So in that sense it is fixed, it lies ahead, it is waiting for you. There will be a notice in the newspaper announcing it, along with the time and place of the funeral. There may even be an obituary, a life in five hundred words with an old photograph that moves those who love you in a way they can't quite explain.

Like the funeral address, the obituary is one of the arts of anamnesis, one of the ways we try to re-present a life before it fades into the past. It's a difficult art. Too many of them concentrate on listing achievements and successes, so they read like post-mortem petitions for a public honour. But just occasionally something of the turmoil of a *lived* life will come through. They are the ones I like, the ones I profit from. I'm not bothered about how many directorships they had, or how many books they wrote and the prizes they won. But I do like to read about their struggles with sorrow or sex or religion. I like to hear how they played the hand life dealt them. I am helped by the knowledge that, behind the confident public face, the private face was sometime streaked with tears.

The obituaries I devour with particular interest are those of the movie stars of my boyhood, though most of them have already gone. My reasons for this obsession are complicated. It is partly because they take me back to the now of then in the picture palaces of my youth, long before the multiplexes and the shiny rows of concession stands in the lobby. Like many children of my generation, I escaped the constraints of a cramped existence by living vicariously through the glamorous characters up there riding across the silver screen. There was a consoling side to this movie habit that was relatively benign. And it was at its most therapeutic during and in the years immediately after the Second World War. We needed an occasional escape from grey reality, and the imaginary world of the movies provided it. But there was an insidious side to it as well, analysed by the film historian Mark Cousins:

> . . . Hollywood films have an emotional amplitude greater than that of everyday life. Dark clouds hang over them as they do in romantic poetry and painting, and their stories are drawn against the background of that fate. Theirs is a phenomenally successful brand of emotional excess . . . [I refer to] as 'closed romantic realism'. I use

'closed' because these films tend to create worlds that do not acknowledge that they are being watched and the actors behave as if the camera isn't there . . .[92]

It was this closed, romantic world that dominated my inner life and its imagined longings when I was a child. Many commentators have remarked on the similarity between cinema goers and the watchers in Plato's *Parable of the Cave*. Plato's watchers face away from the real world outside and concentrate on the hypnotic shadows flickering on the back wall of the cave. It is the unreal that is most real to them, as it was to me. I remember coming out of the dark picture house into the sunlight of the war's double-summertime and feeling bereft that the dream was over. And I wasn't the only one who felt like that. In his poem, 'Cahiers du Cinema', Sean O'Brien captures the sense of expulsion we all felt when the movie ended and we went sadly home:

We watchers in the cave are cast out once for all
Into that fearful teatime light where everything is being filmed
And narrative has given way entirely to its critics, who must
     read
A thousand screens at once for damning evidence of dreams.[93]

Of my generation of dreamers, Joan Didion is the best expositor of the closed romantic realism of the movies we were immersed in during those years. She and I fell for the same characters, John Wayne being the most arche-typal. She started going to the cinema a few years later than me, during the summer of 1943, the year John Wayne starred in *War of the Wildcats*. She tells us that is when she first saw the actor who was known to his friends as the Duke. That's when she saw the walk and heard the voice telling the girl in the picture he would build her a house 'at the bend in the river where the cottonwoods grow'. When Wayne died, she wrote about him in an essay she called 'A Love Song'. It was less an obituary of the actor who had just died of cancer than an exposition of the dreams he had stimulated in those of us who had been watching him over the years.

. . . when John Wayne rode through my childhood, and perhaps through yours, he determined forever the shape of certain of our dreams. It did not seem possible that such a man could fall ill, could carry within him that most inexplicable and ungovernable of diseases. The rumour struck some obscure anxiety, threw our very childhoods into question. In John Wayne's world, John Wayne was supposed to give the orders. 'Let's ride', he said, and 'Saddle up'. 'Forward ho', and 'A man's gotta do what he's got to do'. 'Hello, there', he said when he first saw the girl, in a construction camp or on a train or just standing around on the front porch waiting for someone to ride up through the tall grass. When John Wayne spoke, there was no mistaking his intentions; he had a sexual authority so strong that even a child could perceive it. And in a world we understood early to be characterized by venality and doubt and paralysing ambiguities, he suggested another world, one which may or may not have existed ever but in any case existed no more: a place where a man could move free, could make his own code and live by it; a world in which, if a man did what he had to do, he could one day take the girl and go riding through the draw and find himself home free, not in a hospital with something going wrong inside, not in a high bed with the flowers and the drugs and the forced smiles, but there at the bend in the bright river, the cottonwoods shimmering in the early morning sun.[94]

Didion has captured here what it is that touches me when I read obituaries of my boyhood heroes of the silver screen. What grabs me is the contrast between their idealised existence, their heroic presence on the screen, and the quotidian, often depressing reality of their lives off screen. Didion found it impossible to associate illness with her image of John Wayne. But there was more to his human vulnerability than the cancer that killed him. He was bald. And he must have hated it, because off screen as well as on he hid it beneath a toupee. It was as if he had lost the difference between the movie legend John Wayne and the boy Marion Morrison born in a small Iowa town in 1907. And there was a more profound anomaly than the difference between his idealised physical beauty on the screen and the paunchy, balding man he became in real life. In his films, he always played the courageous and lonely hero who took up arms against the oppressor and his bandit gang. Yet in real life, he managed to finesse his way out of being drafted into the military in the Second World War. He looked like a hero. He walked and talked like a hero. But his heroics were all in the movies. John Wayne was an act. But he wasn't the only schoolboy crush I had whose actual life was very different from the one I saw in the pictures.

A good obituary can capture and explain these contrasts and help us sympathise with the forces that provoked them. After all, the actor is only a heightened version of the tendency in many of us to spend so much of our lives auditioning for roles we fancied that we never fully embraced the one scripted for us. Marion Morrison wasn't John Wayne. He *acted* John Wayne. As do many of us in our own way. And that's fine – as long as we acknowledge the distance between the act and the real thing before it's too late. The tragedy is to die without knowing who you were, to keep the act going till the end. Like the student in a poem by Lynda Pastan who studied so long for life that she woke one morning to discover someone was already walking down the aisle collecting the papers.

The beauty of getting near death is that it gives us a last shot at reality, at owning and admitting our real selves. When I was writing my memoir, *Leaving Alexandria*, I became aware that it had become an extended act of self-examination. I see no reason now to revise the verdict on myself I reached then. Like Peter the Apostle – maybe this is why he moves me so much – I have spent much of my life wanting and sometimes pretending to be the kind of person I admired but wasn't. I think of them as people who don't get in their own way, people who do not appear to bother very much about themselves. What they have in abundance is a capacity for application to the task in hand, whatever it is. They stick at things. As well as being the mark of the saint, this is also the mark of the great scholar. In a word, they possess patience. 'Patience' has the same root as the word 'suffer'. It is the ability to endure not only pain, but boredom, the grind of necessity. I was good at enduring physical pain but bad at enduring dullness and lack of excitement.

It manifested itself as an irritation with the boredom of the small print, the detail of the agenda, and a failure to finish things. Always an enthusiastic starter, I was too impatient to be a good finisher. My life has been littered with attempts to play musical instruments and learn languages and acquire technical understanding of the devices and machines I used without knowing how they worked. None of it was achieved to any level of accomplishment. Fortunately, there were a few occasions when there were people around me who were able to finish what I had impulsively started – and some good was done. The starter impulse is still there, and I occasionally give it a flourish by revisiting an old failure. And I wonder what that was all about. I try to console myself with Isaiah Berlin's parable of the fox and the hedgehog. The fox knows many things, but the hedgehog knows one important thing.[95] The trouble is I am neither fox nor hedgehog. I know a little about many things but not a lot about anything.

I see now that there was something visceral about my impatience, something that was part of my physical and psychological make up. And it had a dark side. It made me a dangerous driver. I had four serious road accidents in my life, all of them my fault. Two on motor bikes, two in cars, for one of which I had my licence removed for a time. My wife Jeannie says my problem is I have a 'driven' personality. It made me a risk taker, impatient with any rules and processes that might slow me down. Even walking on the hills I could never take it easy. I suppose it had some good sides to it. I was an editor's dream. I never missed a dead-line, though my speed could make for sloppy writing. And I was good at chairing meetings, most of which go on far too long and many of which are a waste of time, anyway. Getting there was always the point for me – but where's *there*? And why the rush? I wonder now if I was catching up on myself after a tough start and a patchy education. Was I trying to prove that the Random Street boy could make it – or fake it – with the best of them?

Looking back, what I regret most about the rush is missing so much of my own life. I don't mean missing it now. I mean missing it *then*, missing it while I was in the midst of it. I am sorry I did not pay more attention to the world while I was racing through it, particularly to those who were close to me. I am also sorry I was never the sort of boy who was fascinated by the natural world and busied himself in learning how it worked. I never studied birds or watched butterflies or explored the changes in frog spawn. On the hills, which I started walking as a very young boy, I didn't pay attention to what was actually around me. It was the movement that was important to me, as well as the dreams I was conjuring in my imagination as I strode on. This is the weakness of the romantic temperament. It spends too much emotional energy pursuing the elusive and fascinating other, rather than concentrating on the gift that is actually close at hand. I wish more of my attention had been spent on the 'here' of my life rather than on the 'elsewhere' I was in pursuit of.

Apart from my inherent impatience, I suspect that this tendency always to be looking ahead rather than looking around was intensified by catching the religious bug early.

It diverted me into spending too much time trying to understand life rather than just living it. I was in my head rather than in the world. Rather than learning all I could about the world that enveloped me, a bit of me got diverted into obsessing about where it came from. Before he died a few years ago, I took this question to a philosopher friend I discussed these things with. 'Why is there something and not just nothing?' 'Richard,' he replied, 'there just is. Get used to it!' Not that there has to be a conflict between these two fascinations, between the 'What' and the 'Wherefrom'. I know some who have kept them in perfect balance, fascinated both by the world's life and the mystery of its origins. I never achieved that balance. Now I regret not knowing what I was looking at when I did look at the earth and the creatures it nurtured, including the ones who nurtured me.

That's why I am grateful to old age for slowing me down at last and, in Clive James's phrase, for helping me 'see the cosmic blaze and feel its grandeur' before it's too late. I am also glad I figured myself out before the end, though I wish I'd done it sooner. It would have helped me had I realised earlier that my acceleration system wasn't in sync with my braking system. But it was the life I was dealt, the cards I was given to play. No Saint or Scholar among them, but a few useful ones, nevertheless. And I can say this: whatever else it lacked, my life was rarely boring. Still, I hope I have enough time left at the table to get better at what Nietzsche called amor fati,[96] love of the fate I was dealt, the life that wove itself on the loom, the person I was. Maybe even to love him the way Derek Walcott commanded:

You will love again the stranger who was your self.
Give wine. Give bread. Give back your heart
to itself, to the stranger who has loved you.[97]

The stranger who was yourself and who has loved you?
It's intriguing the way poets are convinced some of us are
destined to get to know and accept ourselves only when
we are close to the final disclosure of death. Michael
Donaghy said almost the same thing in the poem I have
already quoted from:

For the face they now cover
is a stranger's and it always has been.[98]

Befriending the stranger within, the stranger who was
yourself, is an elusive but liberating idea to get hold of.
But it can be difficult to understand. It's easier to grasp
the importance of loving the stranger who is *not* yourself,
though we find that just as hard to do. The Letter to the
Hebrews in the New Testament tells us why we should
try:

Be not forgetful to entertain strangers:
for thereby some have entertained angels unawares.[99]

Fear of the stranger seems to be deep in the human psyche.
Evolutionary psychologists suggest that it might even have
had survival value during the childhood of our species.
Sometimes they *were* out to get us. Wherever it came from,
it can close our hearts and minds to 'the other' and
the good news they could be bringing us. That's why the

unknown author of the Letter to the Hebrews likened them to angels. And it's why the poet Louis MacNeice took the idea further:

> For every static world that you or I impose
> Upon the real one must crack at times and new
> Patterns from new disorders open like a rose
> And old assumptions yield to new sensation;
> The Stranger in the wings is waiting for his cue,
> The fuse is always laid to some annunciation.[100]

The poet tells us to be open to the strangers in our midst or we'll miss their annunciations, the good news they bring us. I get that. What is harder to get hold of is the idea that the stranger who is myself might also bring a gift if I welcome him home. How am I to understand that and act upon it? The clue lies in six words from those lines from Derek Walcott I have already quoted: '. . . give back your heart to itself'.

Those of us who have spent much of our lives wanting or pretending to be someone else have been disloyal to the self we were. Yet another example of the craving the Buddha told us was the source of all human misery, even if it was only the desire to be a different person: someone better looking or cleverer or holier or purer or braver – anyone other than the self we were. That was always impossible, the poet tells us, so before it is too late give back your heart to yourself. Say 'Yes' to the stranger you were. He's been in the wings all your life, waiting for his cue, waiting to be invited onstage. He doesn't mind that you've left it till the curtain is about to fall. He understands that was in the cards like everything else. But there's one last card to play, and he wants you to play it bravely, as yourself.

Just the way the Duke did. It was in his dying that John Wayne finally became John Wayne. At the end he was brave not just up there on illusion's bright screen but in a real hospital on a high bed with the flowers and the drugs and the forced smiles. 'Let's go,' he said. And this time it wasn't a line from a movie. It was an act of personal bravery. Courage can be death's last gift to us, if we'll grasp it.

Another sad romancer who came to himself at the end was my old friend Saint Peter. We have already watched him auditioning for the role of hero in the gospels, knowing in his heart he was a fraud. As they say in Texas, Peter was all hat and no cattle. And that seems to have been his story right up to the end. There is no obituary of Peter in the gospels, no official account of his death. The history books are silent as well. But there is a legend I like because, fiction or not, there is something authentic about its take on the old betrayer. According to the story, Peter was an old man in Rome when the Emperor Nero started to persecute Christians as a cover for his own guilt for the fire that was destroying the city. Again Peter's courage failed him. The legend describes him making his escape from persecution in Rome, trudging along the Via Appia, on the run again. Was he thinking about his three denials that night thirty years before? Did he hear the cock crow as he reached the edge of the city? And did the Lord turn and look at him? This time it was different. This time Jesus walks towards him.

Quo vadis Domine? asked Peter.

Where are you going, Lord?

Eo Romam iterum crucifigi, replied Jesus.

I am going to Rome to be crucified again.

Again Peter bursts into tears. But this time he turns round and goes back to Rome and his own crucifixion. The legend says that when the moment came he asked to be crucified upside down because of his lifetime of desertions. That has an authentic, over-the-top Petrine touch to it, a bit of characteristic swagger. 'Time to face the truth,' he thinks to himself. This time he did. And it didn't matter that it had taken him his whole life to get there. A life takes as long as it takes to bring us to our truth, even if we only make it on our death bed.

I have said it before. I shall say it again. We didn't get to deal our hand in life. We only got to the play the cards we were given. And how we play the last card can win the game. A death well faced can be redemptive of a life that may not have been well lived. There's something of this idea in the Christian and Islamic tradition of the martyr whose voluntary death can purge the sins of a lifetime. A moment of courage at the end can wipe out a lifetime of failure and excess. There is a lot of darkness in the history of the doctrine in both those religions, of course, and it still plays out grimly in today's headlines. But the truth remains that a brave and reconciled death can perfect an imperfect life. It places a full stop on the script. Another story is completed. That's why I read obituaries religiously now; waiting for the period to be stamped onto the last sentence of the last paragraph;

praying that I'll do my own dying well when my last page is turned.

But what has surprised me most about obituaries is that reading them as a regular discipline helps to reconcile me to my own death. They work like those meetings of substance abusers who help each other overcome their addictions by owning and sharing them. Reading obituaries encourages me to confess my own condition. I take my place in the wide circle in the waiting room and say to the others assembled there: 'Good evening. My name is Richard, and I suffer from a terminal disease called mortality. Like all of you in here tonight, I am waiting for the last bus.' It's strangely comforting.

As the days of my years blow away like pages from a calendar in an old black-and-white movie, I know it's maybe not far away, the date of my death. But the thickening fall of all these obituaries reminds me I'll be among friends. Anxiety fades as I recognise that my name has also been enrolled in the great democracy of the dead. Sooner or later the bus will be along for me. But I've been a walker all my life, so when I hear its approach afar off I hope I'll have time to lace on my boots and set out to meet it. I'll try to take it easy this time.

> . . . I think I'll take a road I used to know
> That goes by Slieve-na-garagh and the sea.
> And all day breasting me the wind will blow,
> And I'll hear nothing but the peewit's cry
> And the sea talking in the caves below.

I think it will be winter when I die
(For no-one from the North could die in spring)
And all the heather will be dead and grey,
And the bog-cotton will have blown away,
And there will be no yellow on the whin.

But I shall smell the peat
And when it's almost dark I'll set my feet
Where a white track goes glimmering to the hills,
And see, far up, a light . . . [101]

ACKNOWLEDGEMENTS

This book began its life as a series of broadcast essays delivered on BBC Radio 4 in the slot that follows the One O'clock News. The suggestion for the series came from James Murray, whose company Butterfly Wings Productions Limited produced it for the BBC in January 2016 under the title 'Three Score Years and Ten'. Encouraged by my agent Caroline Dawnay and my then editor at Canongate, Jenny Lord, I used the broadcasts as the impetus for writing this book, and I am grateful to them for their pressure and encouragement. I am also extremely grateful to my new editor at Canongate, Simon Thorogood, for all the care and attention he brought to the editing of the text as it emerged, and I'd like to thank Rafaela Romaya, Canongate's Art Director, for the beautiful cover she has designed for the book.

I am extremely grateful to Marion Goldsmith and Rena Mackay for allowing me to use excerpts from the addresses I gave at the funerals of their husbands, both of whom I remember with deep affection.

I am also grateful to the Niven family for allowing me to use the address I gave at the wedding of Amy and Graham.

I owe my wife Jeannie more than I can find words for, but I am particularly grateful to her for her advice on bereavement counselling, a subject on which she is a practised expert.

I read a lot of poetry, so every poem quoted in this book I have discovered myself – except one, 'Goodbye to the Villa Piranha' by Francis Hope. I found it in Alan Bennett's *Keeping On Keeping On* and knew immediately it would be important to me. I am grateful to Alan Bennett for the discovery.

My dog Daisy died as this book was going through the final stages of the copy-editing process. She was seventeen years old and for every minute of those years she was happiest when she was beside me. We walked thousands of miles together on the Pentland Hills till she was too old and tired to keep up. The first trek I took without her was on Good Friday four years ago. It seemed the right day for it and I wept as I strode through the Green Cleugh without her wee body trotting behind me, close at my heels.

Her final years were of peaceful decline. Slower walks round the block. Having to be carried upstairs. More visits to the vet. Sleeping most of the time, though dogs have always been great at that anyway.

We held her close as the kindly vet released her from what had become a painful disintegration.

ACKNOWLEDGEMENTS

Given how old I am, she will not be replaced. Daisy was my last dog. And the years blow away like leaves in the wind.

RH

NOTES

1 Bede. *History of the English Church and People*. Bk IV, c.13. Translated by Leo Sherley Price. London: Penguin, 1956.

2 Shakespeare, William. *Hamlet*. Act III, sc. iii, 73.

3 Luke 16:9, *Revised English Bible*. Oxford University Press, 1989.

4 Turner, Charles Tennyson. *Collected Poems*. 1880.

5 Binyon, Laurence. 'The Burning of the Leaves'. In: *The Oxford Book of Twentieth Century Verse*. Oxford University Press, 1973, p. 102.

6 Psalm 90:10. In: *Scottish Prayer Book*. Edinburgh: Cambridge University Press, 1929, p. 629.

7 Yeats, W.B. *The Poems*. London: Everyman's Library Classics, 1992, p. 239.

8 Larkin, Philip. *Collected Poems*. London: Faber & Faber, 2003, p. 190.

9 Bruce, George. 'Departure and Departure and . . .' In: Lucinda Prestige (ed.), *Today, Tomorrow: The Collected Poems of George Bruce 1933–2000*. Edinburgh: Polygon, 2001.

10 Hollinghurst, Alan. *The Line of Beauty*. London: Picador, 2004, p. 500.

11 Thomas, Dylan. *The Poems*. London: J.M. Dent and Sons, 1974, p. 162.

12 Glendinning, Victoria. *Leonard Woolf: A Life*. London: Simon and Schuster, 2006, p. 31.

13 Gawande, Atul. *Being Mortal: Illness, Medicine, and What Matters in the End*. London: Profile Books, 2014, p. 187.

14 Horace. *Ars Poetica*. 173.

15 Guinness, Alec. *A Positively Final Appearance*. London: Penguin, 2000, p. 98.

16 Watts, Isaac. First published in *Psalms of David* (1719).

17 Larkin, *Collected Poems*, p. 58.

18 Falkner, John Meade. 'Christmas Day: The Family Sitting'. In: *The Oxford Book of Twentieth Century Verse*, Oxford University Press, 1973, p. 42.

19 Cupitt, Don. *Ethics in the Last Days of Humanity*. California: Polebridge Press, 2016, p. 6.

20 Pascal, Blaise quoted in F.C. Burkitt, *Speculum Religionis*, 1929, p.150.

21 Lewis, C. Day. 'Christmas Eve'. In: *The Complete Poems*. London: Sinclair Stevenson, 1992, p. 517.

22 Letter of John Keats to George and Tom Keats, 1817 (No. 45).

23 Larkin, *Collected Poems*, p. 58.

24 MacNeice, Louis. *Collected Poems*. London: Faber & Faber, 1979, p. 195.

25 Hope, Francis. 'Goodbye to the Villa Piranha'. In: *Instead of a Poet and Other Poems*. London: The Bodley Head, 1965.

26 Hopkins, Gerard Manley. 'I wake and feel the fell of dark, not day'. In: *Poems of Gerard Manley Hopkins*. Oxford University Press, 1952, p. 109.

27 Kierkegaard, Søren. *Notebook IV A*.

28 Eliot, T.S. 'Little Gidding'. In: *The Complete Poems and Plays*. New York: Harcourt Brace, 1952, p. 141.

29 Shakespeare, William. *Macbeth*. Act V, sc. i.

30 Warnock, Mary. Green College Lecture, 1996: http://www.bmj.com/content/bmj/304/6833/1045.full.pdf

31 Romans 7:15–20.

32 Romans 8:28.

33 Calvin, Rev. John. *Institutes of the Christian Religion*. Book 3, Chapter 21.

34 In: Smart, Ninian and Richard D. Hecht, *Sacred Texts of the World: A Universal Anthology*. London: Quercus, 2007, pp. 163–64.

35 Shakespeare, William. *King Lear*. Act IV, sc. i, 48

36 Arendt, Hannah. *The Portable Hannah Arendt*. London: Penguin Books, 2000, pp. 180–81.

37 Jeremiah 31:29.

38 Nietzsche, Friedrich. *Untimely Meditations*. Cambridge University Press, 1997, p. 62.

39 Hopkins, *Poems*, p. 110.

40 St Aubyn, Edward. *Some Hope*. London: Pan Macmillan, p. 378.

41 St Aubyn, *Some Hope*. p. 377.

42 St Aubyn, *Some Hope*. p. 386.

43 St Aubyn, Edward. *At Last*. London: Pan Macmillan, p. 256.

44 Lord Tennyson, Alfred. 'Crossing the Bar'.

45 Donaghy, Michael. 'Exile's End'. In: *Collected Poems*. London: Picador, 2014, p. 216.

46 Hopkins, *Poems*, p. 107.

47 Heidegger, Martin. *Being and Time*. Part 2.

48 Extract appears in Allott, Kenneth. *Contemporary Verse*. London: Penguin, 1950.

49 Lichfield, Gordon. 'The Science of Near-Death Experiences'. In: *The Atlantic Monthly*, April 2015.

50 Holloway, Richard. *A Little History of Religion*. Yale University Press, 2016, p. 12.

51 Lord Tennyson, Alfred. 'Tithonus'. In: Helen Gardner (ed.), *The New Oxford Book of English Verse 1250–1950*. Oxford: Clarendon Press, 1972, p. 655.

52 Tessimond, A.S.J. 'Heaven'. In: Hubert Nicholson (ed.), *The Collected Poems of A.S.J. Tessimond*. University of Reading, 1985, p. 83.

53 Surah 56, 'On the Day of Judgement', the Qur'an.

54 Joyce, James. *Portrait of the Artist as a Young Man*. London: Penguin, p.121.

55 Aquinas, Thomas. *Summa Theologiae*.

56 O'Connell, Mark. *To Be a Machine*. London: Granta, 2017, p. 24.

57 O'Connell, *To Be a Machine*, p. 29.

58 Barnes, Julian. *Nothing to be Frightened Of*. London: Jonathan Cape, 2008, p. 61.

59 Shakespeare, William. *King Lear*. Act V, sc. ii.

60 James, Clive. 'Event Horizon'. In: *Sentenced to Life*. London: Picador, 2015, p. 15.

61 Grassic Gibbon, Lewis. *Sunset Song*. Edinburgh: Canongate, 2006, p. 256.

62 Grassic Gibbon, Lewis. 'Cloud Howe', *A Scots Quair*. London: Hutchinson, 1967, p. 207.

63 Larkin, *Collected Poems*, p. 43.

64 Bennett, Alan. 'Diary', *London Review of Books*. Vol.36, No. 1. 2013.

65 Raine, Kathleen. 'Poem 95'. In: *On A Deserted Shore*. Dublin: Dolmen Press, 1973.

66 Auden, W.H. 'Funeral Blues'. In: *Collected Shorter Poems 1927–1957*. London: Faber & Faber, 1966, p. 92.

67 2 Samuel 18:33.

68 'Order for the Burial of a Child'. In: *The Scottish Book of Common Prayer*. Edinburgh: Cambridge University Press, 1929, p. 468.

69 Auden, W.H. *Collected Poems: In Memory of W.B. Yeats*. London: Faber & Faber, 1976, p. 197.

70 Schwarz-Bart, André. *The Last of the Just*. London: Penguin Books, 1977, p. 373.

71 Work, John W. (ed.). *American Negro Songs and Spirituals*. New York: Bonanza Books, 1940, p. 123.

72 I Corinthians 15:3–8.

73 I Corinthians 15:12–15.

74 I Corinthians 15:51–5.

75 Donne, John. In: Sir Arthur Quiller-Couch (ed.), *The Oxford Book of English Verse 1250–1918*. Oxford University Press, 1968, p. 238.

76 Weil, Simone. *An Anthology*. New York: Grove Press, 1986, p. 163.

77 Stevenson, Gerda. 'Your First Visit to Church'. In: *If This Were Real*. Middlesbrough: Smokestack Books, 2013, p. 46.

78 MacNeice, *Collected Poems*, p. 30.

79 Leopardi, Giacomo. 'Song of the Wild Cock'. In: Miguel de Unamuno, *Tragic Sense of Life*. Translated by J.E. Crawford Flitch. New York: Dover Publications Inc., 1912, p. 123.

80 Larkin, *Collected Poems*, p. 190.

81 Beckett, Samuel. *Three Dialogues with Georges Duthuit*. London: Calder and Boyars, p. 125.

82 Berger, John. 'The Infinity of Desire'. *Guardian*, 13 July 2000: https://www.theguardian.com/culture/2000/jul/13/artsfeatures.art

83 Luke 22:19.

84 I Samuel 28:7–14.

85 Gray, John. *The Immortalization Commission: The Strange Quest to Cheat Death*. London: Allen Lane, 2011.

86 Carrington, Dora. '16 February 1932'. In: *Letters and Extracts from her Diaries*. Cape, 1970.

87 Luke 22:19.

88 'Funeral Service'. In: *The Scottish Book Prayer Book*. Cambridge University Press, 1929, p. 453.

89 *Hymnal for Scotland*. Oxford University Press, 1966, p. 486.

90 Glendinning, Victoria. *Vita: The Life of V. Sackville-West*. London: Weidenfeld & Nicolson, 1983, p. 301.

91 O'Donoghue, Bernard. 'Going without Saying'. In: Neil Astley (ed.), *Being Alive*. Bloodaxe Books, 2004, p. 448.

92 Cousins, Mark. *The Story of Film*. London: Pavilion, 2008, p. 67.

93 O'Brien, Sean. *November*. London: Picador, 2011, p. 17.

94 Didion, Joan. *Slouching Towards Bethlehem*. New York: Farrar, Straus & Giroux, 2008, p. 30.

95 Berlin, Isaiah. *The Proper Study of Mankind: An Anthology of Essays*. London: Chatto & Windus, 1997, p. 436.

96 Nietzsche, Friedrich. *Ecce Homo*. II, 10. London: Penguin Books, p. 68

97 Walcott, Derek. 'Love After Love'. In: *Collected Poems 1948–1984*. London: Faber & Faber, 1986.

98 Donaghy, *Collected Poems*, p. 216.

99 Hebrews 13:2.

100 MacNeice, *Collected Poems*, p. 195.

101 Waddell, Helen quoted in D. Felicitas Corrigan, *Helen Waddell: A Biography*. 'The Mournes'. London: Victor Gollancz, 1986, p. 222.

PERMISSION CREDITS

Author photo © David Eustace

RICHARD HOLLOWAY was Bishop of Edinburgh and Primus of the Scottish Episcopal Church. A former Gresham Professor of Divinity and Chairman of the Joint Board of the Scottish Arts Council and Scottish Screen, he is a fellow of the Royal Society of Edinburgh. *Leaving Alexandria* won the PEN/Ackerley Prize 2013 and was shortlisted for the Orwell Prize 2013. Holloway has written for many newspapers in Britain, including *The Times, Guardian, Observer, Herald* and *Scotsman*. He has also presented many series for BBC television and radio; *Waiting for the Last Bus* originated as a five-part series on Radio 4 in 2016.